FACTION MAN | Bill Shorten's Path to Power

David Marr

THE NUMBERS: 24 TO 26 JULY 2015

By the third afternoon of the conference, the horse-trading was happening
in plain sight. Mobs gathered on the floor of the auditorium. Emissaries
went back and forth. Lone figures looked to their phones for answers. At
the microphone, delegates from the boondocks poured their hearts out
about aged care and the latest notion to defeat branch stacking. No one was
listening. The real interest in the vast, spring-green auditorium of the Melbourne Convention and Exhibition Centre was elsewhere: not on the fate
of gay marriage, the immediate cause of the commotion on the floor, but
on a question that mattered for the entire Labor Party. Was Bill Shorten in
control? So far at the national conference he had won every round. Pundits
predicting his humiliation at the hands of the Left had been proved
wrong, indeed ridiculous. He had had his way even on refugees: Australia
under Labor would stay in the company of the least civilised nations on
earth, pushing refugee boats back out to sea. But could he end the weekend with what he needed to consolidate his leadership of the Opposition:
a near perfect score?

This is a man from nowhere. He built his career out of sight inside the union movement. Had he cut his teeth in parliament we would know him better by now. He became a public figure at Beaconsfield less than ten years ago and only edged into cabinet in the last years of Julia Gillard's government. He has failed to emerge strongly as a leader since. The verdict of the focus groups is mixed. There is no great disagreement with what he does. He seems a safe pair of hands. Yet people still wonder what he stands for. Where Tony Abbott is disliked quite viscerally now that he is known, Shorten is suspect because he isn't. His story isn't familiar. The successful decade he spent at the head of one of the country's biggest unions tends to be dismissed as a job, something he did while waiting to get into politics. He still has a faint halo from the Beaconsfield mining disaster, but he is also the plotter who brought down two leaders to clear his own way to power. The sight of Shorten talking on his phone outside a Chinese restaurant on the night of Rudd's downfall is one of the most remembered images of the man. If remembered at all, his record as a minister in the Rudd and Gillard governments is recollected well. The rape case is closed. He is not thought to be making many mistakes as leader of the Opposition. But he's seen as a shape-shifter, driven entirely by politics. Yet the party is united behind him and nearly every poll taken since Abbott won office suggests Australia would welcome Labor back with open arms under Bill Shorten's leadership.

"We are being transparent to the Australian people," he told the delegates to the 47th ALP National Conference, who gave themselves a standing ovation for being so brave debating difficult issues in the public gaze. When the count was called, the delegates held their passes in the air like schoolkids begging for attention. The place was a garden of dangling red lanyards. And Shorten was comfortably home on pushing back the boats. But he knew that already. He had done what he has so skilfully done ever since he put on long pants: gathered the numbers. The Maritime Union of Australia (MUA) and the Construction, Forestry, Mining and Energy Union (CFMEU) had broken from the Left to deliver him victory. God

Quarterly Essay

Quarterly Essay is published four times a year by Black Inc., an imprint of Schwartz Publishing Pty Ltd. Publisher: Morry Schwartz.

ISBN 978-1-86395-753-3 ISSN 1832-0953

Subscriptions – 1 year (4 issues): $59 within Australia incl. GST. Outside Australia $89.
2 years (8 issues): $105 within Australia incl. GST. Outside Australia $165.

Payment may be made by Mastercard or Visa, or by cheque made out to Schwartz Publishing. Payment includes postage and handling.

To subscribe, fill out and post the subscription card or form inside this issue, or subscribe online:

www.quarterlyessay.com
subscribe@blackincbooks.com
Phone: 61 3 9486 0288

Correspondence should be addressed to:

The Editor, Quarterly Essay
37–39 Langridge Street
Collingwood VIC 3066 Australia
Phone: 61 3 9486 0288 / Fax: 61 3 9486 0244
Email: quarterlyessay@blackincbooks.com

Editor: Chris Feik. Management: Sophy Williams, Caitlin Yates. Publicity: Anna Lensky. Design: Guy Mirabella. Assistant Editor: Kirstie Innes-Will. Production Coordinator: Siân Scott-Clash. Typesetting: Tristan Main.

Printed by Griffin Press, Australia. The paper used to produce this book comes from wood grown in sustainable forests.

knows what debts must be paid. On the list might be "safeguards" for jobs; a seat or two in state upper houses; a place on a trade mission to China; and out on the fringe of one of the nation's capital cities, someone's daughter may become deputy mayor.

That's how it works, and no one works the system better than Shorten. He is a master of the art of negotiation, a deal-maker of immense skill. He betrays without flinching. The career of this man of the Right is proof that Right and Left don't mean much anymore in Labor politics. "I don't hate anyone in the Labor Party," he declares. "It's not a completely amoral world. But you begin to realise over time that Right and Left arguments can get over-cooked." What were once mighty building blocs of the party are now unstable coalitions of the roughly like-minded. At the national conference, the CFMEU deserted the Left on the boats, and next day the National Union of Workers (NUW) broke with the Right to undermine Shorten's position on marriage equality.

He set to work. He is not Bob Hawke, who sat above the fray, relying on his lieutenants to bring him the numbers. Shorten is hands-on. He uses his contacts, deep in the party. He believes they give him a better under-standing of what Labor is thinking than any of his recent predecessors had. He goes right down the line. When he discovered, sometime in the morning, that the conference was shifting against him, he took out his phone. Labor MPs were allowed a conscience vote on marriage equality. Shorten wanted it to stay that way. But the Left was determined to make the policy – like any other party policy – binding on MPs. A collision between him and his deputy, Tanya Plibersek, was looming. He made calls. Faction leaders met. He twisted arms. The horse-trading spilled onto the conference floor. Around 4 p.m. a compromise was hammered out: marriage equality would remain a matter of conscience in this parliament and the next, but become binding on the party thereafter. Shorten pledged to bring marriage reform to the vote within 100 days of taking office. He faced down key opponents, that branch of the Catholic Church known as the Shop, Distributive and Allied Employee Union, the Shoppies. He and

Plibersek put the compromise to the conference in the early evening and it was carried on the voices.

Nearly everything had gone his way over those three days in Melbourne. He had played the numbers superbly. The decks were cleared for the coming elections. His authority in the party had been showcased to the nation. And he could only have shared the relief of old faction warriors that the hours spent on this newfangled marriage policy had edged off the agenda the truly difficult issue facing Labor: rebalancing the power of the unions, the members and the machine. Shorten's career is a product of the great conundrum of the party: the wretched state of democracy within.

Shorten's body is not made for suits. His baggy frame sits on skinny legs. At factory gates in the old days he wore chambray shirts and bomber jackets. There's something about the new uniform of coat and tie that suggests a plugger dressed for court. He has that great asset for a politician: a big, easy smile. But he affects a clumsy, serious face, creasing his brow in what photographers who trail him call "the full wifi." Time and Canberra have taken their toll. In the seven years since he came to parliament, he has aged about twenty. At the time of the Ruddslide he cut a boyish figure. Now there is more head, less hair and not so much of the charm that once swept men and women off their feet. The accent is just right: educated and classless, part Xavier College and part Australian Workers Union (AWU). It's a highly serviceable political package but the question is: does it scale up from party leader to prime minister?

Contenders for leadership can rarely pick the moment to make their run. Shorten needed more time. That's often been the way with him. He has always moved so fast: from rookie union organiser to leader of the Opposition in less than twenty years. He is yet to turn fifty. But he stepped up after Labor's defeat in 2013 without hesitation. He told friends he had no choice: now or never. And he put himself forward knowing history wasn't with him: since World War II no one taking the helm of his party after a great electoral defeat has become prime minister. It's a sad list: Billy Snedden, Bill

Hayden, Andrew Peacock, Kim Beazley and Brendan Nelson. But Shorten believes he can pull off the double, beating history and Tony Abbott.

The conference consolidated his leadership of the party. The press accorded him grudging respect. Had he stumbled, he would have been torn to pieces by the commentariat. News Corp beat him about the head for union links and union power. That was to be expected. Questions were asked on whether Labor would live up to its promise to be brutal to refugees. No surprises there. The recommitment of the party to tackling climate change was met with general respect. And then he and his party had the pleasure of watching Bronwyn Bishop's helicopter ride, Abbott's diehard opposition to marriage equality and Dyson Heydon's dalliance with the Liberal Party do terrible damage to the Coalition.

Ahead of Shorten lies a challenge he's never faced before: an absolutely open contest. Each step of the way until now has been won by deals, faction plays and the occasional walkover. He's as tough a backroom fighter as federal politics has turned up in a long time. A Shorten speciality is a brutal backroom contest that hands him a public victory "unopposed." He is the member for one of the safest Labor seats in the country. He was the first leader of his party to win his position in a ballot. But that was not open either: eighty-six members of caucus had as much say as — and out-voted — 30,000 rank-and-file members of the party. Now Bill Shorten faces the nation.

Another hard rule of the last half-century has been that only larger-than-life leaders bring Labor in from Opposition. Whitlam, Hawke and Rudd were such men. Shorten isn't. But neither is Abbott. In this contest of lesser men, Ipsos, Newspoll and Essential agree that Australians regard Shorten as a great deal more understanding than his opponent, far more broad-minded, steadier and a deeper thinker. But they distrust Shorten almost as much as they distrust Abbott. That's why this election will be fought on trust. Abbott is rehearsing his lines. In a single answer in Question Time in late August he let rip:

That smirking phoney over there, that assassin, the two-time Sussex Street assassin ... Twice this Leader of the Opposition led the Sussex Street death squads to assassinate politically two prime ministers, and then he was caught out telling lies about it on the Neil Mitchell program. That is this person who now seeks the trust of the Australian people at the next election ... We support the workers of this country. Where does this man stand? I tell you: when it comes to dudding workers, that man has form. He wants to dud the workers of Adani, he wants to dud the workers who will be employed under the free trade agreement, but, worst of all, when he was charged with protecting low-paid workers, he ripped them off to help himself. Shame on him.

It's going to be dirty. At the heart of the contest will be Shorten's character. All the way to polling day, Australians will be invited to rake over every detail of his short life and hidden career.

His mother made all the decisions. Ann McGrath came from a long line of Irish Australians. She had two faiths: Catholicism and education. As a young woman teaching in London, she fell under the spell of the Jesuits of Farm Street and determined that any sons of hers would have a Jesuit education. She was thirty and on a cruise to Japan when she met Bill Shorten, the second engineer on the ship. They were very different people. She was teaching at the Townsville campus of the University of Queensland. He was a chain-smoking Englishman who had gone to sea in his teens rather than finish school in Durham. She brought him ashore. When the boys were due, she moved her husband to Melbourne, where he took a job at the Duke and Orr Dry Dock on the Yarra. After the twins were born in May 1967 — Bill was first out — she began her doctorate while her husband settled down to run the dock. She was always studying. He was dealing with the men and their union, the Painters and Dockers. He hired them, drank with them, and was remembered as a boss who knew the way things worked: there were always too many men in the gangs at Duke and Orr. But that was the deal. The work got done and strikes were rare. Years later he would tell the Costigan Royal Commission into the Federated Ship Painters and Dockers Union: "I have suggested to many people in the past to get a better record you would have to go to Russia or China."

The boys were university brats, parked in day care at Monash and roaming the corridors in their holidays. In time, their mother became a lecturer in education at the university. They lived nearby, in the unprosperous streets of Murrumbeena. She and the boys went to mass each week. Their father never did. Her faith was firm but not unquestioning. She believed in thinking things through for herself. She told her boys to do the same. When they came to her with questions, she said: "Look it up." A new priest came to Sacred Heart when they were nine. Father Kevin O'Donnell would turn out to be one of the most appalling paedophiles ever sheltered by the church. Ann didn't care for the man. She wouldn't let her sons be altar boys. They went to the Polish mass each week. Why, they asked. "Because it's quicker and I like the priest."

They didn't see much of their father. Bill's life was the dock and the men. He was around at the weekends, smoking with a beer in his hand. He took his boys to the football and let them play at Duke and Orr, which was on the riverbank beside the site of the Melbourne Convention Centre. Sometimes he brought the men home. Shorten remembers the union secretary, Jack "Putty Nose" Nicholls, coming round to the house with Pat Shannon, who was shot dead in a South Melbourne pub when the Shorten boys were only six. His father worked with a tough crowd. He never learnt to drive. Shorten says he owes his people skills to his old man. His mother was the brains and drive. She was a woman of incredible determination: the first of her Ballarat family to win a scholarship, the first to go to university. The McGraths, the Nolans and the O'Sheas had come out to the diggings in the 1850s. They were unionists on all sides. "There was politics in her family," Shorten said at his mother's funeral. "Uncle George was a Communist Party member. Grandpa wanted to be but was too scared of Grandma." Ann became a teacher, helped her siblings through university, and then kept studying. She travelled the world and was almost over the hill before she found her husband. There were only the boys. She demanded a lot of them and didn't approve easily. "The breadth of her formidable intelligence should not be underestimated," said Shorten. "Perhaps that was her challenge. She would not suffer fools. She was never rude but she had little time for people who didn't try or who supported unsupportable views, little time for fatuous, superficial humbug. She would be annoyed with people who kept women down. Gossip bored her."

Though De La Salle College offered the twins scholarships, Ann held firm to her resolution and delivered them to Kostka Hall, the junior school of Xavier College, in 1977. Xavier was a school for rich Catholics, but the Shorten boys were not the only ones whose parents both worked to pay the fees. That did not make them intruders. Among the well-heeled clientele of the Jesuits, there survived respect for parents doing what the Shortens were doing: vaulting their kids straight into the professions. "This, from the beginning, was one aim of Jesuit Education," wrote the order's revered superior general, Pedro Arrupe, on the occasion of the school's centenary in 1978. But he directed Xavier to do much more: to turn out "men-for-others." Arrupe's mantra played out in rather different ways across Jesuit Australia. As the Shorten boys arrived at Xavier, Tony Abbott was leaving Riverview, its sister school in Sydney, as a committed warrior in Bob Santamaria's fight against the Red Menace and the collapse of Western civilisation. But Xavier was a different place. The school wasn't fighting the modern world tooth and nail. Vatican II was accepted.

"Don't let your heads be turned," Ann Shorten told her sons. They did the things small boys do in schools like this: athletics, debating and theatre. In the 1979 Gilbert and Sullivan revue, Robert was a pirate and Bill a fairy. Robert's star shone a little brighter than Bill's. They weren't much alike: Robert was taller, better-looking and darker. His achievements on the track were applauded, while Bill earned praise for his "outstanding contribution" to St Paul's School for the Blind in Kew. By this time, the Shorten boys were at the school's main campus, with its chapel as big as the cathedral of an Italian hill town. Kew was a long haul – a tram and two trains – from Neerim Road, Murrumbeena, but they didn't scurry home. Bill ran the box office for the 1983 *Romeo and Juliet*, played the piano, endured elocution lessons, fenced and played cards: bridge at Xavier but later five hundred. Shorten's love of cards – of bluff and bidding – is a key to the boy and the man. Only in his final year did he outshine his brother as a debater; he was chosen for the state team in the national championships of 1984. Though they finished third, his friend John Roskam was generous in the *Xaverian*: "William proved a credit to the College." None of this made him a memorable figure. His headmaster, Father Chris Gleeson, remembers him as neat and polite. "He was always in a suit, always with his tie done up. He kicked around with very quiet, well-behaved young men. He did nothing of moment at the school. But he was a fine debater and a capable student."

Shorten and his friends gathered round the Roskams' television to watch Bob Hawke defeat a stricken Malcolm Fraser. "We were all very excited by the Labor victory," recalls Roskam. "Hawke was new, fresh and bringing us together. Hawke in '83 was like Rudd in '07 for the young: a fresh start." At sixteen it was already clear Shorten was heading for politics. This was an unusual goal for a Xavier boy at this time. The school turned out surgeons and judges, not politicians. He says his first ambition was simply to be in parliament. He knew he could debate. Though not a natural leader in the Xavier mould – he was never a prefect or house captain – he would not accept defeat in an argument. "The house meetings for this year will long be remembered as Bill Shorten's battle-ground," reported the *Xaverian* in 1984. "His speeches were truly a marvel." The school voted Liberal, but Labor was the only possible party for the boy. Labor was the default setting of his family. He was the grandson of union men on both sides. His mother never turned her back on the Labor world of her Ballarat childhood. And in his final year at school, Shorten fell under the spell of his Australian history teacher. The parents might have been snobs at Xavier, but the teachers weren't.

"I've always been a Labor supporter," says Des King. "I'm rusted-on. But I never saw myself as promoting the Labor cause. It wasn't like that. The classes I taught were fair-minded. I wasn't indoctrinating them. I tried to be balanced." He remembers how smart Shorten was: quiet and smart. There was no bombast about him. King remembers how Shorten lapped up his lessons on the 1890s depression, the shearers' strike, the rise of Labor and the early triumphs of federation. "I taught for a long time and taught a lot of boys. He'd be in the top half-dozen students I ever taught." But what set Shorten apart in that school were his politics. "Bill stood out because he always expressed a Labor point of view," says King. "He always did."

At some point in his final year at Xavier, Shorten tried to join the party. He heard nothing back. So he took himself off to see his local member, Race Mathews, who quickly straightened things out at the branch for this impressive young man. "He is breaking his neck to work for the party," thought Mathews. "He is precisely the sort of young man we want to bring into the party and the party needs." Shorten's membership came through on 3 March 1985.

Xavier left him with an undogmatic faith; a modest swag of prizes; a slight lisp; a close acquaintance with the rich; and political ambitions. At the Year 12 dinner, a drunk Bill Shorten senior fell asleep at the table. It was mortifying. He was drifting out of their lives. Most of the twins' Xavier friends were off to the University of Melbourne but their mother's preference was Monash. She was about to complete another degree there – this time law – with great distinction. She boasted: "I was a very embarrassing mother." Not really. Shorten says: "I chose to go to Monash University because Mum was there."

From the moment he arrived at the age of seventeen, he threw himself into the political fray. He now claims, "I wasn't really that involved in campus politics." That's rubbish. At Monash Shorten became a star of the Labor Right. He was elected almost at once to the Public Affairs Committee of the Monash Association of Students, and had no sooner joined the Fabian Society than he began campaigning to be president. The student newspaper *Lot's Wife* reported:

> Our spies also spotted contenders for next year's Club Presidency, Bill Shorten and Luisa Bazzani, buying drinks for anyone that showed the slightest inclination to sell their vote at the annual general meeting. We believe that Luisa stitched up John Fetter's vote with a Bundy'n'Coke and four helpings of the main course.

Shorten won. He had joined the ALP Club the moment he stepped onto the campus, and battered away for years at its entrenched leadership. The ALP Club stayed stubbornly Left. When the club put this terrier last on its list of candidates for the new Victorian Union of Students, he outwitted them with the slogan "Vote up the ticket." It's a victory he still boasts of today. Even as a fresher, Shorten was able to pluck out of the air Minister for Defence Robert Ray for an earnest campus debate on taxation policy. And then he reported the night for the student paper:

> In reply to one question as to why the family home shouldn't be subject to the capital gains tax, Robert Ray replied: "expediency, pure expediency". Thank god for common sense in political animals!

Shorten would dazzle students over the years by bringing big Labor names to Monash: Paul Keating, Neville Wran, West Australian premier Brian Burke, and even the prime minister, Bob Hawke. He seemed to know them. More to the point, they seemed to know him. This early meeting with Ray at Monash mattered: in a few years he would become the senator's apprentice.

From the start Shorten was looking beyond Monash. He was taken under the wing of an older student, Michael Borowick, now the assistant secretary of the ACTU. Borowick saw campus politics as a way of feeding students into the youth wing of the Labor Party. "The Socialist Left had successfully used student unions to recruit for their faction the best and brightest of left-of-centre students," he explained to the *Sunday Age*. "So I decided we would do the same thing and establish an infrastructure at a campus level that would recruit the best and brightest of a moderate persuasion." In young Shorten he found an extraordinarily talented recruiter. That was his genius. He gathered a tribe around him at Monash and walked them into Young Labor, where he and Borowick set up a faction eventually called Network. Aaron Patrick wrote in his book *Downfall*: "Network had one primary objective: to crush the Left. The corollary plan, which Shorten didn't spell out because he didn't really need to, was to launch his political career."

Patrick, now the deputy editor of the *Financial Review*, was one of Shorten's converts: "Bill was just the best recruiter there has ever been. 'You must recruit, recruit, recruit,' he would say. 'The numbers are everything.'" Soon Shorten was recruiting across the campuses of Melbourne. His orders were: "Get all your mates into Labor. Go to the conferences. Court the unaligned and the waverers." He never stopped. Face to face he was irresistible. He swept men up in his wake. "If he wasn't fighting you," Roskam recalls, "he was trying to convert you." The two school friends found themselves at times in league against the Left. University Liberal clubs were drawn into these wider manoeuvres. So was the Australasian Union of Jewish Students. The cause of Israel united the Right. Shorten loved intrigue. He fizzed with ideas but moved so fast that other people were left to make them happen. He wasn't great on detail. His brand of politics was fun. "It was about getting normal people into politics, not dour lefties, not freaks," says Peter Cowling, who became Shorten's right-hand man in these early years and is now an executive with GE. "Bill was the life of the party. His key skill was getting people involved. He was 'natural as' talking to anyone. He was charismatic. From extremely early on it was clear this bloke was going into politics and he was going to be senior."

Shorten moved out of home early in his time at Monash. There were rough share houses, great parties and many girls. He earned his way cleaning trays in a butcher's shop. Stephen Conroy was first sighted by this crowd in a grubby house Shorten was renting in Carlton. Jason Koutsoukis, who knew both men, recalls Conroy packing down for games of hall rugby: "A sport where five-a-side teams would battle it out in a corridor a metre wide, trying to get a rugby ball from one end to the other." Conroy had arrived in Melbourne in 1987 to be Robert Ray's lieutenant. A kid from Britain who never lost his accent, Conroy proved to be a master of the dark arts of party warfare. He was only a couple of years older than Shorten. They were wary of each other at first, but in time formed a tight alliance that lasted twenty years until it came unstuck over the execution of Julia Gillard.

Shorten was a figure of fun for the Monash Left. He was mocked as "Private Bill Shorten" for briefly joining the university regiment. (His official parliamentary biography records "Military Service: Australian Army Reserve 1985–86.") Pairing hit songs with campus identities one year, *Lot's Wife* nailed Shorten with Carly Simon's "You're So Vain". Xavier was already being held against him. Derided as a snob in the student paper, a wounded Shorten fought back:

> In your last edition … I was misquoted as claiming there is no dignity in pushing a shovel. This was a vicious, irresponsible and demeaning article. To put the readers straight I would like to clarify what I said … I do not believe that the unemployed should have to work for the dole nor should they be forced to do so. Hence, there is no dignity in pushing a shovel or any other work which the unemployed are compelled to do. Hopefully, there will not be too much misquoting of important issues in the future. Having spoken for five minutes I was disappointed to see two seconds of my speech reported. If anyone is further unclear as to what I meant then please see me …

That winter, at a conference described as "a festival of faction fighting" peppered by "spiteful screaming matches," the Network team took control of the policy and administrative committees from the Left for the first time. It was a coup that advertised the talents of Borowick and Shorten to the elders of the party. It was 1986. At some point that year, Network held a camp at Portarlington on the western side of Port Phillip Bay. Out of the blue nearly thirty years later, as he was about to become leader of the Opposition, Shorten was accused of raping a woman at the camp. He denies having sex with her.

Shorten went part-time. There was so much to do, so many new faces to recruit, so many marches to lead up Spring Street. Big issues were in the air: apartheid, Palestine, abortion, AIDS, famine in Africa. They didn't get much attention on campuses. More pressing for students was the Hawke government's decision to reintroduce tuition fees. Enthusiasm for Labor was hard to maintain in universities in the late 1980s. Shorten managed. But politics at Monash was proving disappointing for him: he never scaled the heights of the student association; a coup attempt at the ALP Club failed dismally; and he was dogged by taunts about Xavier boys and shovels.

He began to lend a hand in Senator Gareth Evans' Melbourne office. Shorten found the Minister for Transport and Communications smart and generous but distant. "I know they say that the Hawke government was drifting by then, but I thought they were doing plenty. I just thought it was really interesting to be at the periphery of how politics works." Shorten was kept busy assembling a database of Labor voters. The Left worried about the civil liberties implications of this novelty. Shorten defended the project in *Lot's Wife* as "legitimate market research" available only to members of parliament. Evans gave the Network kids their only remote claim to a policy success. Young Labor was calling for Sydney's Triple J to become a national network. Peter Cowling had taken up the issue. Shorten backed him: "We lobbied Gareth very hard." An audience was arranged for young Cowling. Evans heard him out. Their part in the ultimate result is impossible to assess, but Triple J went coast to coast. Shorten says: "That was something real."

After John Cain's government was returned for the third time in late 1988, Shorten was employed as youth affairs adviser in the office of the new industrial relations minister, Neil Pope. This was a job. He had a wage. He abandoned campus politics and disappeared from the pages of *Lot's Wife*. Shorten swears there was more to his appointment than access to stationery, phones and faxes to recruit for Network. "No. No. I was a youth affairs advisor. Brian Burdekin brought down his report into homelessness. I worked on the state Labor government's responses. I worked on the youth employment program with Steve Bracks." But Network also flourished. This was the year Bob Hawke came to dinner and Shorten became president of Labor's Youth Policy Committee. And at the end of 1989 he travelled for the first time: to Berlin just after the Wall came down (he has a souvenir chunk), through East Germany and into Czechoslovakia, backpacking – for the most part on his own – and sleeping in youth hostels.

He didn't return to Monash for a year. Network was pursuing an audacious plan that went badly – no, humiliatingly – wrong: to seize control of the small, poor, left-wing Victorian branch of the Australian Theatrical and Amusement Employees' Association (ATAEA). This was not about improving the lot of the ushers, gatekeepers and carpark attendants the ATAEA represented. It was meant to prove to the bosses of the Right faction that Network's leaders were ready for big things in the party. Suddenly university students were working as ushers at Flemington. Aaron Patrick reports them preparing for the onslaught: "They spent a couple of days in eastern Victoria at a training camp working on strategies. Law and economics students from Melbourne's top private schools role-played speaking to poor, older men." The old guard of the union slaughtered the students, and in the shakeout that followed, a good deal of anger was directed at Shorten. After years of infatuation, friends broke with him forever. Some look back to their time in his tribe with amused resignation, some with bitterness. In 2013, Christina Cridland wrote in Perth's *Sunday Times*:

> As a former Young Labor leader said to me at the end of our time in Shorten's Young Labor group, Network: "Young Labor is very good at taking idealistic young people and turning them into Machiavellian mother------" ... while my initial involvement in Young Labor was motivated by idealism, most of my time ended up being spent as a pawn for the "king of the kids", as Shorten was known. That is, helping Shorten outnumber the left wing of Young Labor, and even a rival sub-faction of the right wing of the youth party, which was led by Shorten's now close mate and senator David Feeney and another enemy-turned-ally, Andrew Landeryou.

All his life Shorten has left behind people who feel betrayed by him. He denies casting people off when they are no longer of any use. He insists he keeps in touch, even now, with old campaigners from university and the union. But there have been so many new best friends over the years. "You can't keep in touch with everyone," he says. "I get that there is disappointment amongst some people. They look at me and say, well, he's here and I'm there, and what happened?" Many he's dazzled and dumped understand. They recognise that the intimacies formed in political brawls are intense but may not outlast the campaign.

But the complaints about Shorten that saw him walk away from Network were different. Close allies discovered he was dealing with the enemy. Shorten had recruited his followers with a simple appeal to work with his team in the Right against the whole world. But he was looking further down the track, beyond the light opera of smashing the ATAEA. He had a career to consider. "Politics," he says, "is a long-distance race, not a sprint." Some of this was about leaving the amateurs behind and drawing close to the most professional of his rivals: Stephen Conroy, David Feeney and Melbourne University activist Richard Marles. It was a tough but shrewd move. His old friends would happily have gone with him, but Shorten was working behind their backs. That was the betrayal that powered the split of 1990. "We were cheesed off," one explained, "because he was doing it all for Bill."

He returned to Monash to finish his degree. His mother had mandated he must be admitted as a solicitor. That meant finding a perch for a few years in a legal firm. At Slater and Gordon he was interviewed by a young leader of the Left in Victoria, Julia Gillard. Twenty-five years later she wrote: "I enjoyed his cheeky demeanour, was impressed with the spirit of endeavour that seemed deeply ingrained in him and said in the interview, 'We should offer you a job.'" But he found articles elsewhere, for which Bob Kernohan claims the credit. Kernohan told the Royal Commission into Trade Union Governance and Corruption:

> He was active in Young Labor … as an older bloke looking at the young fellow, I thought, "This bloke has ability. He's nearly finished his law degree." He was very keen to get involved in my planned campaign in the AWU. I asked Bill if he would be my campaign manager. He was more than happy. In fact, he was relishing the opportunity to become my campaign manager.

Shorten was doing chores for Robert Ray when he fell in with Kernohan. It would prove an unhappy meeting. Kernohan was battling to regain his place in the AWU leadership with the help of the boss of the Victorian Right. His solicitor was John Cain, son of the just-retired premier and the senior partner in the leading Melbourne Labor firm Maurice Blackburn and Co. "John Cain Junior talked to his partners," said Kernohan. "They put Bill on."

The young man concentrated, in a rather distracted fashion, on the injuries of working men and women. "From the time he commenced, it was clear his interest was not in personal injuries," says Peter Koutsoukis, who supervised his work. "He wanted to deal with the unions." But he had a remarkable knack. "He was very good at convincing clients to sign up to litigation. That isn't easy." In December 1993, a ten-seater de Havilland Dove clipped four houses in Gilbertson Street, Essendon, before coming to earth in the garden of a fifth. No one was killed. But Shorten recruited seven residents to sue the owner of the plane, Ted Rudge of Rudge Air. Koutsoukis was impressed: "He went out holding sort-of public meetings and going door to door and signed up a lot of people." The case made the *Age*: "A lawyer with Maurice Blackburn and Co, Mr Bill Shorten, said yesterday that the legal action was the largest group claim for nervous shock taken in Australia." The firm settled in the end. "But Bill signed up a lot of people to cost agreements."

Kernohan was accusing the AWU leadership in Victoria of gross neglect of duty. He had Shorten give the details to the *Australian*, the *Age* and the *Financial Review*: "Mr Kernohan said that in 18 years as an AWU member he had 'never seen the Victorian AWU in such a mess.' He believed it faced a deficit in 1991–2 of nearly $1 million." The newspaper clippings were turned into flyers sent to every member of the union in Victoria. In the face of this campaign, the AWU's Queensland boss, Bill Ludwig, installed his protégé, Bruce Wilson, as acting state secretary in Victoria in mid-1992. Wilson was seen as a man with a big political future. But he was grossly corrupt, milking a slush fund he'd set up in Western Australia using money from the construction giant Thiess. His lover, Julia Gillard, had done the paperwork for the fund at Slater and Gordon. The tangled Wilson story would cast a shadow over her prime ministership and leave a permanently disgruntled Kernohan accusing Shorten of failing to pursue the miscreant and his ill-gotten gains.

The young man's time at Maurice Blackburn was odd and brief. "He advised our senior lawyers on how to deal with the media – what should be the angle, what was a good grab," says Koutsoukis. "I remember him going to Channel 9 with some of our senior lawyers one day to advise them. He showed remarkable acumen in this at a young age." Shorten's advice was always the same: "Where someone has been badly hurt or badly done by, you've got to talk about their story." Koutsoukis says he was a player in a great coup for the firm: "He helped us build relationships with unions. He assisted us in recruiting AWU as a client. Bill played a role in that, advising on the politics behind it, and he knew key individuals."

After eighteen months at Maurice Blackburn, his obligations to his mother fulfilled, Shorten looked for a way into politics. By this time, he had come to regard the secretary of the ACTU as his mentor. "He was very young and still a university student," recalls Bill Kelty. "But genuine Labor." What did he teach the boy? "The experience of experience itself." Shorten gave it all a rather courtly air in his maiden speech to parliament: "When I was a young and green solicitor learning about workers compensation from John Cain Jr, at Maurice Blackburn, Bill invited me to join the union movement." Shorten had set his sights on the AWU. Kelty wasn't encouraging: "I told him, 'It's a basket case. By all means go in, but it's going to be a battle.'" The ACTU chief advised him not to be one of those private-school boys who go into unions as industrial advocates: he should go in as an organiser.

"He was very ambitious in all things," says Koutsoukis. "He always had his eye on being secretary of the union and knew the best way to get there was to be on the shop floor and mix with the members. Industrial advocates only get to know the members in disputes. Organisers get to know them all. This was a deliberate strategy to put him on the path to becoming secretary." Even at the age of twenty-seven, Shorten was making no secret of his higher ambitions: "He used to say he would be prime minister one day."

Shorten sat in the witness box like a boy outside the headmaster's study. On his face was apprehension and disbelief. He blinked a lot. On the footpath nineteen floors below were the same camera crews that had staked out the Independent Commission Against Corruption when Liberal officials were flayed in 2014 for funnelling hundreds of thousands of dollars in prohibited donations to the NSW branch of their party. Now, a few blocks across town, it was Labor's turn. Shorten's appearance before the Royal Commission into Trade Union Governance and Corruption was early at his request, made in the hope that he could cut through the gathering media narrative of Shorten the corrupt union boss. He swore on the Bible.

Abbott promised a royal commission into the unions if he won power, and they gave him plenty to work with while he was in Opposition. Millions were found to have been stolen by officials of the Health Services Union (HSU). That scandal, still unwinding, left a former president of the Labor Party behind bars. The union's former national secretary, Craig Thomson, was disgraced and fined, and escaped prison only by the skin of his teeth. Meanwhile, Gillard and her government had been dogged by the squalid tale of Bruce Wilson's AWU slush fund and the suggestion that she had benefited from his frauds. In early 2014 the Fairfax press published allegations of corruption, standover tactics and links between bikie gangs and the construction division of the CFMEU.

Abbott announced his royal commission a few days later "to shine a great big spotlight into the dark corners of our community to ensure that honest workers and honest businesses get a fair go." He talked crime but the terms of reference he gave the former High Court judge Dyson Heydon AC QC did not limit the commission to hunting for criminals. At least as urgent was investigating money flowing from employers to unions. These payments come under dozens of guises – some legal and some illegal – but they all cost industry. They boost union power. They bleed into the coffers of the Labor Party and they exasperate the Liberal Party. The search for ways to turn off this tap never ends. Shorten was in the box to answer for deals done on his watch which had won the AWU hundreds of thousands of dollars.

Why were the deals done, asked counsel assisting the Royal Commission, Jeremy Stoljar SC. And were they done at the expense of the AWU rank and file? "Instead of securing better wages or penalty rates for members, some officials may have preferred to obtain benefits which strengthened the Union balance sheet and which falsely inflated membership numbers."

Shorten had fumbled his response to the announcement of the commission. His rhetoric was all over the shop. He sided too strongly with the unions. He didn't make a firm and early commitment to cooperate. That he was a target was never in doubt. In a profound breach of convention, the incoming government was using its power to investigate – and if possible disgrace – its predecessors and rivals. Rudd was put before the Royal Commission into the Home Insulation Program. Gillard and Shorten would face the trade union commission. As it happens, Rudd emerged little damaged from the former, and Gillard was given a clean bill of health by Heydon. But Shorten's standing suffered the moment the commission was announced. It fell further in May 2015, when Stoljar turned his attention to the AWU.

Cesar Melhem, an AWU official turned politician, was forced to resign as government whip in the Victorian upper house when Stoljar revealed a company called Cleanevent Australia was paying $75,000 in AWU dues each year while the union was apparently allowing it to strip casual cleaners of penalty rates worth about $6 million. Melhem was Shorten's protégé, his right-hand man and successor as state secretary of the AWU. The deal Melhem struck had been cancelled as soon as it was discovered by the man who took over from Melhem. "I thought it was untoward," Ben Davis told the commission. He ended other similar deals: "I think employers paying membership dues on that scale profoundly weakens us in the workplace."

As Shorten waited to appear before the commission, the papers filled with complex stories not quite suggesting illegality in his dealings as an AWU boss. Abbott was on the airwaves denouncing employers for "dudding their workers as part of a sweetheart deal with the unions." His concern for lost wages and conditions was heartwarming. News Corp's sudden enthusiasm for penalty rates – after decades of campaigning against them with ferocious determination – was profoundly comic.

The Shorten show on 8 July opened with a crowded house of lawyers, journalists, union officials and old political allies. Former ACTU boss Greg Combet sat in as an adviser to the leader of the Opposition's legal team. Mingling with the crowd were beautiful security guards in good suits. We were all safe. Heydon looked almost as ancient as the Duke of Edinburgh. He spoke rarely but with patrician courtesy. His head was often in his hands. On his face through much of Shorten's testimony was fierce disapproval. By the time Stoljar had thrown all he had at the leader of the Opposition, the commissioner seemed exasperated. Shorten had tried his patience. That was clear. But there was something else on that very old lawyer's face that looked a little like impatience with his own mission.

Stoljar landed a serious blow in the opening hours of his examination. He revealed that Shorten had failed to declare $54,742 in political donations for the 2007 federal campaign. After that, Shorten's presence in the box began to seem low-rent. What he had to answer for matters, but was hardly on the scale of the great questions royal commissions are usually rolled out to answer. Did Australia pay kickbacks to Saddam Hussein? Why did Esso's Longford plant explode? Are the churches sheltering paedophile priests? Nothing of this moment was in issue as Stoljar worked over the ground covered by the *Fair Work (Registered Organisations) Act 2009*. Witnesses may yet be brought to contradict Shorten. He may be called back to give further evidence. But in this appearance in the box he was not taxed with committing crimes. Stoljar has accused officials of other unions with corruption, standover tactics and blackmail. He spent his hours with Shorten pursuing conflicts of interest.

Shorten rambled. "There is no way I can answer your question without giving you context." He queried Stoljar's assumptions. He gave stirring accounts of deals done for his workers. He painted pictures: "I don't know if you want me to just very briefly describe a mushroom shed?" He represented himself as an official so busy, so above the fray, that he left nailing down details to everyone below him. He checked little: "I don't micromanage every detail of every administrative arrangement." Melhem was his very busy number two. Employers paid unions for many things – workplace training, advertising in union magazines, paid education leave, tables at union dinners and even union dues – but he insisted that was not evidence of a conflict. The benefit was mutual. And as far as he knew, everything paid for had been delivered by the union. "I would never be party to issuing any bogus invoices, full stop."

The questioning slowed to a crawl. This was by design. Had Shorten's legal team wanted him to answer with a brisk yes, no or maybe, he would have done so. As leader of the Opposition, he was addressing the campaign against him from the witness box. He was honing grabs for the evening news and educating the commissioner in the ways of the AWU. And like all politicians who find themselves before royal commissions, he was displaying the formidable skill they acquire in public life for not quite – or simply not – answering the question. As Shorten danced around the details of payments of $100,000 a year by Thiess John Holland to the AWU, Heydon stopped the witness in his tracks, put his head in his hands and spoke almost kindly:

> You, if I can be frank about it, have been criticised in the newspapers in the last few weeks, and I think it is generally believed that you have come here in the hope that you will be able to rebut that criticism, or a lot of it. I am not very troubled about that, though I can understand that you are, and it is legitimate for you to use this occasion to achieve your ends in that regard.
>
> What I am concerned about more is your credibility as a witness and perhaps your self-interest as a witness as well. A witness who

answers each question "Yes", "No", "I don't remember", or clarifies the question and so on, gives the cross-examiner very little material to work with. It is in your interests to curb these, to some extent, extraneous answers.

Shorten continued, as chatty as before. Rather than growing angry as the day wore on, Heydon grew more polite. Perhaps he'd given up. Perhaps he'd come to think the failings of the leader of the Opposition were small beer. A little before 3 p.m. on the second day, Stoljar sat down. Heydon thanked Shorten. "You may or may not have to come back," he said. "Every effort will be made to accommodate the least inconvenient possible time for you, in view of your responsibilities." At this point it seemed Heydon had many months of work ahead of him. The following week in Canberra he would be getting into the rough stuff with the CFMEU: phone taps and threats of violence and a former official, Fihi Kivalu, being carted off to jail charged with two counts of blackmail. The commission would be earning its keep.

Shorten held a brief press conference round the corner outside a shop selling ugg boots. He knew the danger he was in: people don't follow the details. They just get the flavour. Whether the commission found anything against him hardly matters. The vibe was there: this man's past is shady. He can't be trusted. "This hurt him," says Bill Kelty, who watched the live stream of Shorten's hours in the box. "I rang him afterwards and said to him: if you want this job, there is something called pain. To be prime minister you have to absorb the pain."

The AWU was a shot duck. One of the oldest and biggest unions in the country was bleeding members and wracked by internal division. Its industrial clout was all but gone. After a century at the heart of the Labor Party, its political influence was in steep decline. Several state branches were broke. Only Queensland was strong. It was still a 1950s union. What had seemed a useful merger with the Federation of Industrial Manufacturing and Engineering Employees (FIMEE) was turning into a marriage from hell as officials fought over the spoils. And the ground rules had changed. "The old AWU wasn't up for the times," says Shorten. "We moved from centralised wage fixation to enterprise bargaining. That meant organisers had to do more than just turn up in the tea room. You had to bargain. You had to advance. You had to know how you get negotiations done." The outlook was grim and the opportunities for an aspiring politician endless.

Shorten was put to work doing what he did best: recruiting. The union discovered that this young solicitor who looked like Harry Potter in a bomber jacket compelled attention on the factory floor. He was unfazed by rejection, astonishingly persistent and could talk to anyone. These were his father's gifts. Within a year he was boasting that he had helped recruit 800 new members for the AWU. "A lot of people talk about recruiting," he told the papers. "I would like some of the high-ups in the union movement to try their hand at it." Another talent was swiftly apparent: winning the attention of the press with a string of boutique campaigns. The *Age* reported Shorten signing up greenkeepers and strappers; the *Australian* had him leading a walkout of tomato pickers, which threw the 1996 harvest into chaos; and the *Age* covered his campaign to recruit ski instructors in the Victorian alps. The national jockeys' strike of January 1997 made him a minor figure in Melbourne's imagination. Premier Jeff Kennett backed the jockeys. The industry copped higher riding fees. Shorten told the *Age*: "We are all very excited about the unprecedented cooperation between the AWU, leading trainers and the VRC to promote a cleaner racing industry for stable hands, trainers, owners and the public." The Spring Carnival of 1997 was undisturbed by industrial action. The winner of the cup was Might and Power.

At the age of twenty-eight, Shorten was already kicking the tyres of Maribyrnong. He was living in Ascot Vale, just outside the old Labor stronghold. When a bizarre little scandal known as the Sandwich Shop Affair dragged down the sitting member, Alan Griffiths, Shorten thought he had a show. The Left and Right had been stacking for months, anticipating the fall. Feeney, Marles and a bunch of Young Labor acolytes gave him a hand. But he was effortlessly outmanoeuvred by the man he would eventually dislodge from the seat: Bob Sercombe. Shorten pulled back swiftly. "It wasn't doable," he says. "I didn't have the numbers and I wasn't ready. I hadn't had enough life experience."

After only eighteen months as a recruiter, Shorten was elected to the union's Victorian executive just as Bruce Wilson's frauds came to light. Instead of being sacked, Wilson was paid a handsome redundancy to get him out of the way. The Queensland AWU boss, Bill Ludwig, alerted the National Crime Authority and went to court to try to stop the payments. It was too late. The AWU began to splinter. Bob Kernohan — by this time president of the Victorian branch — was of the faction that wanted to sue Wilson for the money. He would complain all the way to Heydon's royal commission that Shorten was deaf to his plea:

> Shorten cut me off, not in a nasty way, and he said words like, "Bob, think of your future. There's been a pay-out, we are all moving on."
> I said to Shorten, "What, sweep it under the carpet like everyone else seems to have?" Shorten put his hands on my shoulder and responded, "Bob, think of your future." He said, "If you pursue this, a lot of good people will get hurt and you will be on your own. Look, Bob, you've been lined up to take a safe Labor seat of Melton in the Victorian Parliament."

Shorten denied this but the commissioner believed Kernohan. "He has had every reason to remember the event," Heydon wrote in his 2014 interim report into the AWU. "He is therefore much likelier to have remembered the event. He has nothing to gain from his testimony. On the probabilities it is likely that the incident took place as Robert Kernohan narrates it." Kernohan's single-minded pursuit of Wilson saw him cold-shouldered and abused by members of the AWU. He retreated from the union, suffered a nervous breakdown and abandoned plans to enter parliament.

Melton was handed to Shorten. After three years in the union he was in despair. He had been on the losing side of a quixotic attempt to unseat Ludwig in 1997. Ludwig survived easily. That skirmish had done nothing to resolve the internal warfare rife in the AWU. Shorten thought: "Do the people here want to spend the next four years fighting each other or are they interested in getting on with the business of representing members?" Steve Bracks was one of several Labor figures who urged him to switch to state politics. Melton was a tough stretch of Melbourne way out on the road to Ballarat. His preselection was announced in February 1998. He rented a flat in the electorate but never left town. At this point he was approached by AWU shop stewards and asked to become state secretary. Deals were done. The cantankerous old secretary, Bob Smith, was shuffled off to the Legislative Council. At the age of thirty-one, Shorten won the union's top job in Victoria unopposed. Throwing Melton away was a gamble. His political future within Victoria was assured: "Steve Bracks said to me after the '99 election: do you know, if you'd stayed at Melton you'd have been a minister?" These days Shorten calls it a road not taken. There are those who remember him reflecting at times: "I could have been premier of Victoria."

Shorten took over as state secretary in the winter of 1998. Officials were sacked. He cleaned up the office. Financial controls were imposed. He hired accountants and recruited young organisers. He found he had a knack for healing broken institutions and managing difficult egos. "I listen to people," says Shorten. "I'm respectful. People don't have to agree on everything to have a point of view which is worth considering." He set about building trust: "You work at keeping your promises to people over time." He calls the aim "relationship trust," where leadership operates not by individual transactions but through a sense of shared values. He culled the union's deadwood:

> You don't necessarily go around with a chainsaw, but over time you set standards and you ask people to measure up to them. Some people decide that's not what they want to do, or they go look elsewhere. You create new currency. You make merit the currency rather than longevity or just a sort of conservatism. It takes a while but it's not an infinite process.

He took the AWU back into Trades Hall after five years in the cold and began to navigate the factions, cutting deals to stop other unions eating the AWU alive. And he was deliberately militant. He stacked on strikes and he won them. Kelty's advice to him was: "You've got to be a moderate union leader. That means increasing productivity. But you've got to be tough. You've got to have a fight." He kept recruiting and within six months was claiming the union had 18,000 members in Victoria. Netballers and chicken farmers were signed up. Every win and every strike was reported in the press. The new state secretary was always available to reporters. He gave good quotes. He honed his rhetoric at factory gates, on the back of trucks, at the end of wharfs. He is still at his most eloquent on the stump.

Soon after midday on 25 September 1998, Esso's gas plant at Longford exploded. Two men were killed. Eight were injured. The fire burnt for two days. The plant was left a smoking wreck. For three weeks Victoria was without natural gas. Esso blathered. Briefed by AWU delegates at the site, Shorten was able to talk to the media with authority. He was quoted everywhere. As he would discover later at Beaconsfield, being the trusted voice in a catastrophe wins public respect. The first profiles were written. *Business Review Weekly* declared this young man a budding chief executive from beyond the mainstream:

Trade union officials have to be seen as long shots in this selection but Shorten, who is working on an MBA and who spent his early years as a workers' compensation lawyer, has impressed key members of corporate Australia. "I'm the only trade union official in my MBA class, but that won't always be the case," he says. "The union movement needs a range of skills."

When the premier, Jeff Kennett, called a royal commission to investigate the explosion, Esso tried to blame one operator, Jim Ward, for the whole disaster. The commission found Esso entirely to blame for failing to train its operators to deal with the crisis. Ward was given a medal. Esso was fined $2 million. Shorten was all scorn: "Esso makes $1 million a day out of Bass Strait. Suffering fines of $2 million is the equivalent of a corporate speeding ticket for this company."

*

Many women had shared Shorten's life. For some years Nicola Roxon was his partner. He met Deborah Beale in his MBA class at Melbourne University. She was the daughter of Liberal politician and businessman Julian Beale. The pair were engaged in September 1999. She was a futures trader at Merrill Lynch. Her friends vouch for her as funny, down-to-earth, independent and rather more left-wing than him. A few weeks before their wedding in March 2000, she persuaded Shorten to reconcile with his father. They spoke for the first time in nearly ten years. He died a week later.

The Protestant Beales saw their daughter married at St Mary's Catholic Church in West Melbourne at a wedding described in the papers as "a mixture of blue-collar and blue-blood." Marles was best man and Feeney a groomsman. Shorten told the *Herald Sun*: "It's like bringing the Montagues and the Capulets together." Among the 200 guests at the reception were the new premier of Victoria, Steve Bracks, and the cardboard king of Australia, Richard Pratt. Shorten was entering a world familiar from Xavier but he was no longer an observer. He was welcomed. He charmed them.

Not least of his recommendations to this crowd was his naked ambition. He had already turned down a state seat and was clearly aiming higher. His father-in-law praised him to the *Herald Sun*: "The first thing on our minds is that Bill looks after our kid, and he's doing a terrific job ... He's got what we Aussies admire – drive, ambition and dedication. He cares for people and he cares that people have a job, often at the expense of short-term gain." The young couple bought a big house in Moonee Ponds. Most Australians only know the suburb from old Barry Humphries jokes. But the point for an aspiring Labor politician was this: it lies in Maribyrnong. Shorten still had his eye on that prize.

He made peace with Bill Ludwig. This was seen as a great betrayal by those who had campaigned with Shorten only a few years before to bring down the Queensland AWU boss. But it was a shrewd political move that opened the way in April 2001 to his election – again, unopposed – as national secretary of the union, with Ludwig as its national president. Unprecedented was the decision to allow Shorten to keep his old post in Victoria. For the next six years his platform would be national but his power base was Melbourne. The climb from recruiter to national leadership had taken a mere seven years. He was only thirty-four. *BRW* magazine reported: "Shorten, who is called 'Golden Boy' by his staff, says he wants to make the union function better nationally and to devise strategies, such as training programs, that will make the union less reliant on members' dues."

Shorten was good at raising money. He pursued new ways of persuading employers to pay from the moment he took charge in Victoria. He was not the pioneer of these deals but he chased them with determination and suc-cess. His leverage was moderation. Under the new system of enterprise bar-gaining agreements (EBAs), companies and unions could negotiate pay and conditions between themselves so long as workers were left no worse off than they would have been under industrial awards. Each EBA had to pass the famous "no disadvantage" test. What an EBA with the AWU offered was a reasonable deal and certainty that it would be honoured. Shorten could set the tariff high – especially with construction companies – because his union was not the CFMEU. A deal with him could keep rogues and stand-over merchants off a work site altogether, or else make them accept pay and conditions set by the AWU. Shorten told the Royal Commission of a Thiess John Holland negotiator who grew so frustrated with him one day that he protested: "You're asking for so much we could just have the CFMEU."

Shorten struck many deals in his time with the AWU that involved employers paying the union. He insists they were all within the law but won't vouch for the details of every single one: "Whilst I was a very active Secretary, you don't check every clause, you don't line up every pay rate, you rely upon your staff to do it." Some companies paid their workers' union dues. If they want to be members and know they're members, such deals are not illegal. Shorten talks of tidying up these arrangements when he arrived, but he did not end them. He wanted the members. "What profoundly weakens Union organisation is when no one is in a Union," he told the commission. "I make it very clear I support people paying themselves because I think that the more that people directly pay for a service, the more they engage in the quality of it. But in a beauty parade, union or non-union, I guess the union is better." Members are power, explained counsel assisting the commission, Jeremy Stoljar:

> Generally speaking, union membership has been declining in recent years. Someone who can achieve increased membership is bucking the trend. It looks good. Such increasing numbers can give legitimacy to a union's industrial objectives in a particular negotiation or across an industry as a whole ...
>
> Increased membership can also increase the influence of a particular Branch or Division within the Union's National organisation ...
>
> Inflated membership numbers increase the entitlement of that Union to delegates at the ALP National Conference which in turn leads to greater influence over ALP policy formation, greater influence over membership of powerful ALP committees and, in particular, greater influence over the selection of ALP candidates for political office.

Stoljar questioned Shorten for many hours about EBAs he struck with companies willing to sign workers up to the union and at times even pay their dues. He was looking for evidence that these willing recruiters were more gently handled by the union in EBA negotiations. Backpackers and students hired by Cleanevent to clean up football grounds and racetracks joined the AWU by the thousand. Stoljar wondered if membership was essentially automatic: "Are you able to say whether or not there was ever an arrangement in place whereby employees had to tick a box on job application forms to opt out of union membership if they wished to do so?" Shorten claimed not to remember. "I might well have aspired to an opt-out arrangement," he told counsel assisting. "But I honestly don't know." What aroused Stoljar's interest was an EBA struck in 2004 that essentially wiped out weekend penalty rates. Shorten admitted that the EBA was registered with the Australian Industrial Relations Commission without declaring those cuts. The gap between the award and the rates paid by Cleanevent widened even further in the 2006 agreement negotiated by Shorten. Under the award, casuals were supposed to be paid $33.67 an hour on public holidays, while the AWU was happy to see Cleanevent pay them $14.24. In the witness box of the Royal Commission, Shorten insisted that in the real world this was what such casual cleaners were paid:

> If you and I, in 2004 or 2005, were to go out to a fairground or a dog track or a racetrack and find everyone there receiving double time and a half plus a casual loading, to me is fanciful in the real world … it would be great if everyone was getting the Rolls Royce rates which you are asserting, but I have to say in the real world that evidence isn't there.

The Cleanevent EBA was cancelled in 2015 at the request of the present leaders of the AWU, who argued the deal was contrary to the public interest. They assured Fair Work Australia it would be "highly unlikely that any employee would have any objections to the agreement being terminated."

Shorten proved an innovator. He persuaded the Packer family's Consolidated Press to smarten up the *Australian Worker* and sell it on newsstands. Among stories of fresh awards, job threats, historic achievements and tributes to retiring organisers, the *Women's Weekly* of the union movement carried big ads for super funds, Maurice Blackburn and employers of AWU labour. "Nothing untoward about that," Shorten told the commissioner. "Unions have been asking employers and supporters of employers to put ads in their union journals since union journals were printed."

One of Shorten's happiest inventions was the annual AWU ball at Crown Casino in Melbourne. Officially black tie, it brings 800 or so union delegates together for a swanky night of splendid food, big-name comedians and political grandstanding in the Palladium ballroom. Gough Whitlam addressed one of the early shindigs. "This is," he remarked in his sombre drawl, "a long way from the shearing shed." Each year, Labor premiers and prime ministers, presidents of the ACTU, treasurers and MPs gathered in what came to seem, more and more, an act of homage to Shorten, the new man of the Labor Right. Here was the kicker: employers paid for it all. "If the company is willing to pay for its delegates and their partners to get dressed up and have a night out, again, I don't see anything untoward," Shorten told the commission. "Quite frankly, I wouldn't be doing my job if I was asking workers to pay for their own tickets."

The big money came from "paid education leave," which Shorten was one of the first union leaders to import from North America. As he explained to the commission: "It was the idea of a levy, a paid education levy, which would be provided by the company, some small per capita nominal amount which could be used for the training of employees and workers to improve the quality of workplace relations." In late 2001, the AWU was asking employers for five cents for every hour worked by each union member. The companies pushed back. "I had a lot of trouble necessarily going to employers getting them to agree to this," confessed Shorten. "Some employers were happy to pay just for user paid services.

Some employers didn't want to pay for any training and would resist it. Some were happy to come to seminars, and I did get a few to have paid education."

Cash began to stream into the AWU from 2002. Over the next three years, glassmaker ACI, the chemical giant Huntsman International, Chiquita Mushrooms, glassmaker Potters Industries, cleaning supplier Cognis Australia and concrete reinforcing company Ausreo Pty Ltd paid Shorten's union over $650,000 for education leave. Though usually struck during EBA negotiations, these deals were not put in writing and not registered with Fair Work Australia. Stoljar asked:

> Isn't this really the position, that the paid education income simply went into the consolidated revenue, if I want to use that expression, of the Union, and could be deployed for whatever the Union saw fit?

Shorten insisted the money was spent on training, that paid education leave was not secret – he was making speeches about it and delegates could see the benefits in the workplace – and it did not raise conflicts of interest: a better educated and skilled workforce meant more profitable and competitive companies. "They have to be sustainable. The best way you create sustainable companies, which is therefore in the best interests of their employees, is you improve productivity, or, put more bluntly, it's when you can try and find a win/win in industrial relations." Paid education leave was legislated out of existence by the Howard government. There has been no appetite for its return.

*

Standing in an empty paddock on Ferntree Gully Road, heckled by protestors, Steve Bracks turned the first sod for the biggest city road project in the nation. For thirty years, planners had wanted to run a freeway down from the eastern suburbs of Melbourne to Frankston on Port Phillip Bay. Bracks had quashed the idea when he came to office; revived it; faced down fears about birds and wetlands; reneged on a promise not to have tolls; and awarded the project to a consortium that included construction giants Thiess and John Holland. The 45-kilometre freeway plus spaghetti junctions would cost $2.5 billion and take three years to build. At the sod turning in March 2005, Bracks named the project EastLink.

The AWU's EBA with Thiess John Holland was registered a few days before the ceremony. Shorten negotiated it personally. The deal had been reported widely in the Melbourne press. "Tollway workers to earn $100,000" was the headline in the *Age*. Wages would rise 14 per cent over three years. Construction would continue through weekends, with employees able to choose when to take rostered days off. The consortium was happy. Shorten was proud. An angry CFMEU tried and failed to have the Australian Industrial Relations Commission bust the deal. "It was a big proposition," Shorten told the Royal Commission. "I was very interested in terms of making sure we got the best possible deal for the AWU workers on that site. Once I'd done that, then organisers and delegates and other people would get in behind that and do a lot of the day-to-day work of the Union representing its members."

Two months after Bracks dug that sod, the AWU issued the first of a series of invoices which would see Thiess John Holland pay the union exactly $100,000 plus GST in each of the three years it took to build the road. This part of the deal was neither canvassed in the *Age* nor mentioned in the EBA. It was tracked through invoices produced at the Royal Commission. Shorten said: "I cannot speak to invoices specifically issued after my time and, indeed, invoices issued during my time." Some of the emails between the union and the consortium set out how the "agreed sum" of $100,000 was to be paid:

> AWU ball   50 @ 125 = $6,250
> Australian Worker   4 @ 7500 = $30,000
> Sponsorship of AWU OH&S conference 12/8/2006 $25,000
> OH&S training for HRS reps on EastLink $38,750
> Total $100,000.

No suggestion was made during Shorten's two days before the Royal Commission in July that these payments disadvantaged workers on the project. No evidence was produced to contradict Shorten's boast that the EBA he negotiated was "a very good agreement." What puzzled Stoljar was the payment of precisely the same sum each year for three years.

> STOLJAR: Did you discuss with Mr [Stephen] Sasse, who you were negotiating with on behalf of John Holland, a proposition pursuant to which $100,000 would be paid per year with reference to an organiser?

> SHORTEN: No, that is not my recollection and, furthermore, the services which I charge for, which the Union charge for, in my time, could always be explained by reference to functions performed, for training delivered, and this is entirely sensible workplace relations.

As this essay went to press, Sasse had yet to give evidence. Stoljar took Shorten through the bills: what about a $30,000 plus GST charge for "research work done on Back Strain in Civil Construction Industry" in early 2006? Was that work done?

> SHORTEN: Back strain ... is a huge issue in civil construction and heavy industry.

> STOLJAR: I wasn't asking whether it was a huge issue. What I am asking you is, in the period leading up to 18 January 2006, was research work done by the AWU Vic. in relation to back strain?

> SHORTEN: I can't say, I don't recall it, but I believe it would have been if the invoice is issued.

> STOLJAR: Well, the Royal Commission has issued a notice-to-produce seeking records relating to this research to the AWU Vic. and nothing has been produced.

> SHORTEN: If that's what's happened, that's what's happened.

STOLJAR: Well, does that suggest to you that if any research was done, it didn't culminate in a report or the like?

SHORTEN: No. It just suggests to me that the AWU can't find the research.

None of the invoices was signed by Shorten. Every penny appears to have been declared in the union's accounts. There is no suggestion any of it was siphoned off for anyone's personal use. The money was used to make the union strong. The invoices continued to be issued and paid well after Shorten handed the state presidency of the union to his sidekick Melhem. The last of the $300,000 plus GST wasn't paid until EastLink was open for business – under budget and well ahead of schedule – and Bill Shorten was in parliament.

One night in July I watched Shorten on the stump at the Sussex Street headquarters of the NSW Labor Party. It was cold in the courtyard. There was beer and champagne. Old union banners hung from the walls. Faction heavies had gathered for the event. Senator Kim Carr of Victoria was there, looking rather like the headmaster he might have been had he stuck to teaching. Standing at a microphone in the shadows, Shorten let them have it. He was good:

> I believe that Australians are hungry for greater meaning, for a bigger story than fear of the future, fear of the unknown, fear of the different. Australians are smart and they should not be underestimated by this current government. Australians are now organising their lives for this marvellous twenty-first century we live in. They are preparing for the big shifts . . .

These were his people and he spoke to them with the passion of a revivalist. He knows he does this well. But he seems to mistrust eloquence that comes so easily. He distrusts his union voice. He's taken coaching from time to time since becoming leader. He wants to sound different. "I was a union speaker for fourteen years but I've got to have more styles than just that," he says. "It's not about changing the substance. You've got to take some of the rabble-rouser out of you. I think it's about making what you say accessible to people, and people won't always want one gear in a speaker, they want a range of gears."

He can do a fine set speech. His budget replies in both 2014 and 2015 did their work. But so often his efforts are laboured. His big vocal gestures are forced. When he strives for significance it doesn't come off. And waiting to pounce is Shaun Micallef. "A lot of what he says has an imposed gravity," says the leader of the *Mad as Hell* team. "It's as if he's closing the book and declaring the conversation is at an end. But it's not quite the final word it needs to be, to *be* the final word."

Mad as Hell broadcast the first "Zinger" in September 2014. "It was my co-writer Gary McCaffrie's idea to give what Bill says the shape of a Zinger," says Micallef. "Some were jokes and attempts at epigrams we stumbled across on YouTube or on the news. There was a really nice one likening the budget to the *Titanic* with barnacles that had to be scraped off before the ship could be relaunched — the *Titanic*, relaunched? Barnacles?

"There was a grab of him on a loudspeaker in Adelaide shouting about submarines. Give it a hard cut at the end and it sounds like a joke. You can do that with almost anything he says."

The *Mad as Hell* team is ruthless. They harvest Zingers from stumbling words and stumbling delivery. "He speaks with a cadence that suggests a set-up and a punch-line," says Micallef. "It has the grammar of a joke but they really aren't jokes. Gary thought of providing the box for them — the intro and the outro — to give what Bill says the shape of a Zinger. He thought it would be nice to end with a hard cut and a lion's roar … It became a thing."

I'D LIKE TO TEACH THE WORLD TO ZING

ANNAPURNA HIEROGLYPH: That the Titanic was never rebooted or de-barnacled doesn't get in the way of that being a fucking classic. But jokes like that don't write themselves; believe it or not, someone actually thinks them up.

Cut: interior of room — day. Bare except for a desk with computer, a chair and a whiteboard. Pictures of Oscar Wilde, Noel Coward, George Bernard Shaw, Groucho Marx and Kathy Lette line the wall. A writer, Simon Frotting, talks to Annapurna as they watch an old small portable TV (TV's back to us).

ANNAPURNA (*voice over*): This is former *Full Frontal* writer and now current chief speechwriter for Bill Shorten, Simon Frotting.

The audio from the TV he's watching can be heard.

SHORTEN: Once upon a time I thought denial was a river in Egypt. It's actually the attitude of the Abbott government.

SIMON (looking up pleased): That's one of mine.

Jump-cut through some shots of Simon typing, sitting at his desk bouncing a ball off the wall and catching it, opening a Xmas cracker and reading the joke (which he likes and writes down).

ANNAPURNA (*voice over*): Simon spends up to thirteen hours a day crafting his boss's Joke For The Day. Simon also doubles as Labor's head of policy development, so he has plenty of time on his hands.

Cut: Simon at whiteboard, where we see a number of scrawled sentences. Simon takes Annapurna through these.

SIMON: OK, so we've got a couple of examples here: "Tony Abbott: beautiful one day, gone the next." That's if Abbott happens to be in Queensland when the leadership spill happens ... and a variation: "This lame duck just had his goose cooked."

Annapurna smiles politely; Simon is defensive.

ANNAPURNA: From a barely thought-out idea scrawled on a whiteboard to the ears of thousands of Labor voters all over Australia, we see the awesome power of words ... (*She wanders off on a walk, across the path of Shaun at his desk.*) ... words delivered almost but not quite in the right order and sometimes even mispronounced or left out entirely. True satire then is about challenging the paradigm and changing minds, not about silly made-up character names. (*beat*) Annapurna Hieroglyph for *Mad As Hell*.

Politicians speak like their leader, and from the other side of the House, Malcolm Turnbull has watched the Labor front bench over the last year or so master the art of delivering the Zinger:

It is like a bit of chewing tobacco. They roll it up against the top of their mouths, they roll it around their cheeks, their pupils dilate, there is a straining expression reminiscent to anyone who has had experience with young children and then – boom! – out it comes! A literary Exocet aimed at the heart of your victim!

An almost forgotten word was back in the language. Aficionados collected lists of Shorten's best efforts. Widely regarded as among the finest are:

These people opposite are the cheese-eating surrender monkeys of Australian jobs.

Treasurer Hockey ... should just go down to Bunnings, not Bunnings, go to Kmart or Target, buy himself a white tea towel, put it on a wooden broom and wave surrender on his silly changes.

If I can borrow from *The Castle's* line: if anyone thinks that Tony Abbott did this because he cares about the health system and he won't try again, tell 'em they're dreamin'.

We have now arrived at a situation where Tony Abbott's more likely
to visit Greenland than Queensland.

> SIMON: Obviously the trick is not to make the line
> too funny.

> ANNAPURNA: Why's that? Surely—

> SIMON: You see, these lines aren't meant for you
> and me. They're for Mr and Mrs Ordinary Aus-
> tralia — and the thing about Ordinary Australians
> is, they don't like a smartarse. They don't like
> someone who thinks they're funny. Not that I'm
> having a go at your show; Bill's a big fan of *Mad as
> Hell*, particularly your "Bill's Zingers" segment. He
> knows it's done with affection.

> *As Simon turns to the board, Annapurna turns to the camera
> and shakes her head to indicate we're not being affectionate.*

Over Christmas drinks for the Press Gallery, Shorten declared 2014 the
Year of the Zinger, with *Mad as Hell* focusing the attention of the nation on
his metaphors. "Which is pleasing, because all of us put a lot of work into
them, whether it's writing them, delivering them or explaining them
afterwards." In March 2015, the show was nominated for a Logie in the
category Most Outstanding Light Entertainment Program. It was up
against *The Voice* but hopes in the Micallef camp were high. They approached
Shorten, who agreed to pre-record an acceptance speech. He wrote the
words. Micallef directed the shoot. They pulled it off in a single take.

> *An office. Day. The leader of the Opposition is flanked by flags.*

SHORTEN: Hello, everyone. As an unofficial member of the *Mad as Hell* cast, I take great pride in accepting this award on behalf of the show. Frankly, I'm as surprised as you it won. I much prefer some other show whose name I just can't remember. But when Shaun first approached me and the other writers about this project we had no idea how successful we were going to be.

He is handed a Logie. His expression is unflinching, a mix of triumph and hurt pride.

So, thank you. I'm going to keep this for myself. I don't see why I should give it to Shaun Micallef. After all, I've been writing half of his material. And anyway he has been giving it to me for the last couple of years.

Lion's roar.

And the winner was … *The Voice*.

Shorten is still at it, says Micallef. "But there are fewer now. We struggle to find them. I don't flatter myself that I'm responsible for this." Will *Mad as Hell* continue to put Zingers to air? "If they are given to us, it is our duty to continue. But it's up to Bill, not up to us."

BRUTAL MATHS: 2000 TO 2006

"If you finally think you understand it, you've really missed the point."

– Irish saying

They found Greg Wilton dead in his car at 9 a.m. on a remote road in the bush. The Commodore was running. Its lights were on. After a terrible couple of months, the Labor member for Isaacs had killed himself. His marriage collapsed when he was sprung having an affair in Canberra. Weeks later, he was disturbed in another stretch of Victorian bush with his kids in the car, rigging a hose to the exhaust. Police were considering charges. It was all over the papers. He checked himself into a psychiatric hospital in Geelong, but left to live with his sister. She insists the last straw was an article in the *Herald Sun* reporting the manoeuvres already under-way in his faction to dump him: "And the last words that Greg said … were about his so-called mates in the ALP desperately trying to take his job off him." Wilton drove alone into the Yarra Ranges, found a spot on the Tea Tree Track and reconnected the hose. This time it worked.

After a day of tearful condolence speeches in Canberra celebrating Wilton's knockabout virtues and the perils of public life, faction warfare erupted in Victoria. They do politics differently there. Wars are fought in the name of peace. Explosives are packed under the foundations of the Labor Party in the name of stability. They call the wreckage left after these brawls rejuvenation. The wonder is that Victoria delivers any Labor talent to Canberra and remains, decade after decade, a stronghold of the party. Long before Wilton's death in the winter of 2000, the factions had ceased fighting over policy. All that was at stake in the conflicts that had shaken the party for over a decade were places in parliament. In no other party and no other state has so much political blood been spilt for half a metre of leather. Unexpected preselection contests are the most vicious. The conflict is swift and brutal. In caucus, Stephen Conroy was blamed for planting that *Herald Sun* story to promote the candidate he, Shorten and

Feeney wanted for Isaacs. Conroy denied the charge. "How low can these animals go?" Mark Latham wrote in his diary the day of Wilton's funeral. "Hounding a bloke already in deep shit."

Shorten didn't invent the system. He mastered it. In the early years of the new century he came to learn everything he needed to know about courtship and betrayal, deals and numbers, to make him a power in the factions. If he were ever to become Labor leader, he had to turn the machinery to his advantage. The war in the Right that began over Isaacs would see the factions in Victoria splinter; put the careers of Steve Bracks and Kim Beazley into play; distract Labor in two federal campaigns; and end with Shorten's translation to Canberra. It was tough. He suffered at this time some of the few setbacks of his career. But these were the years in which he consolidated his authority in Victoria and the party beyond. The player became the master of the factions. He still is.

A little history: first there was the Split and then the Intervention. "It was the beginning of a golden age for Labor in Victoria," recalls Race Mathews, now retired to his books in a house by the Yarra. "Those were good years to be in the party if you were serious about politics. Victoria leaned more Left than the rest of Australia, but the Left had no hegemony. It was a very lively and interesting party where the grassroots mattered, where there were spirited debates in the branches and party conferences." But the new rules that came with Whitlam's intervention in 1970 had a downside: "The formation of the factions."

Officially there were three: Labor Unity on the right, the Independents in the middle and the old trade union push rebranded the Socialist Left. The labels are confusing: Labor Unity was a byword for bitter division, and the Socialist Left had abandoned socialism and its old dream of bringing down capitalism. Those dreams had lingered into the 1980s, when Hawke persuaded his bitter enemies in the party to back the Prices and Incomes Accord and then – under threat of a second intervention – compelled Labor in Victoria to allow the return of the big unions that departed with the Split. Their arrival at the 1985 state conference of the party at

Coburg Town Hall, with the president of the Musicians Union up in the gallery playing the last post on his clarinet, was a magnificent occasion: "As right-wing delegates arrived at the conference they were met by screaming abuse, jostled, punched and pelted with tomatoes. The brawling continued into the conference hall with some delegates scuffling on the floor and tomatoes being hurled across the room ... scuffles, screaming and tomato throwing continued as party officials struggled to maintain order."

That was the year young Bill Shorten joined the party. With rank-and-file membership falling away, the manoeuvres of the factions were becoming more urgent. Rules introduced to bring democracy to the party fifteen years earlier were being gamed expertly by both sides. Branch stacking was rife through the Labor suburbs. The Svengali of the Right was portly senator Robert Ray, whose chief lieutenant was Stephen Conroy. Andrew Clark analysed the art of Conroy in the *Financial Review*:

> His opponents use words like thuggish and bullying, but Conroy adopted a Stakhanovite approach to the task of factional organisation. He soon dominated Labor branches in the seat of Gellibrand, then spread his influence throughout the state. Conroy was not an originator, but he quickly honed the skills required in the brutal world of factional politics: recruiting new faction-friendly members in key branches, cutting deals across factional lines, flattering waverers, shoring up allies and intimidating enemies.

The bonding of Conroy and Shorten in the 1990s shifted the plates under Victorian politics. Together with David Feeney, by this time state secretary of the party, and Richard Marles, who had become ACTU assistant secretary, the men formed a new subfaction called the ShortCons. It has had – and continues to have – a big impact on national politics. In the late 1990s, this band of brothers set about winning a cut of the spoils in Victoria at the expense of the smooth old warrior who ran Labor Unity for years. The struggle between Greg Sword and the ShortCons broke into open warfare when a candidate had to be found to replace poor Greg Wilton in Isaacs.

Sword was boss of the National Union of Workers. He was the great pioneer of fundraising from employers. The NUW was cashed up and well organised. It had clout. Then along came Shorten, whose revival of the AWU threatened the place of the NUW in the industrial scheme of things as the big, tough but sensible, blue-collar union. "They were the industrial pack leaders," says Shorten. That was until he came along. "I think in my time at the AWU the space wasn't filled by just one union on the Right side of Labor politics." The rivalry of the leaders was intense. Some speak of hatred between them. According to the press at the time, when Sword found the ShortCons pushing their own candidate for Isaacs, he threatened to have Feeney sacked. Sword is said to have told Conroy: "If the NUW is going to be fucked over, if there is going to be a war between us, then David will be the first casualty." The ShortCons blinked. They agreed to back Sword's candidate. But so public had this stoush become that the national executive of the party intervened and Isaacs was given to a local woman with no factional backing, Ann Corcoran. Hers was to be a short career in Canberra. A false peace was brokered within Labor Unity that saw Sword elected national president of the ALP. He was already state president. Shorten was the favourite to succeed him.

Power in Victoria meant finding allies on the other side of the aisle. Unlikely alliances were key to the mastery of the factions. Shorten was courting the "new militants" of the union movement, led by a rabble-rouser called Craig Johnston, whose specialty was leading raiding parties of balaclava-clad unionists through factories and offices. In Bendigo one of these "run-throughs" saw the tires of every car in the factory carpark slashed. At Skilled Engineering in Box Hill in the winter of 2001, Johnston's AMWU (Australian Manufacturing Workers Union) mob broke through the front door with a crowbar, smashed computers, tore pictures from the walls, let off fire extinguishers and terrified the staff. With national elections only months away, Labor leader Kim Beazley was deeply embarrassed by this outbreak of union thuggery. But when the law threatened, Shorten went into bat for Johnston, joining delegations to plead on his behalf to Bracks and the ACTU secretary, Greg Combet. They were ignored. At an ACTU event in June, Shorten manoeuvred Johnston and a group of "new militants" into a photograph with Beazley. He and Combet were furious, fearing the photograph would be used as a bargaining chip to compel their support for Johnston, who was charged, a couple of days later, with riot, affray, criminal damage and aggravated burglary. At this, Shorten backed off, apologised to Beazley and lent his support to calls for a new code of conduct on picket lines. He declared: "We recognise unions need to be strong and militant at times and vigorous on picket lines but not violent and not unlawful." The *Age* mocked the idea of a code. What might it say? "How about simply: 'Keep the peace?'"

Sword, determined to block what seemed Shorten's inevitable rise to the state presidency in June 2002, pulled off a daring faction play. He took the NUW out of Labor Unity and into a pact with the Socialist Left. Driven by little more than Sword's hatred of the ShortCons, this "modernisation alliance" gave the Left mastery over the Victorian party for the first time in a decade. Vengeance was in the air: Feeney was sacked as state secretary; Marles lost preselection for the seat of Corio; and Shorten lost the race for the state presidency. For the first and one of the last times in his rise to power, Bill Shorten hit a wall. His rivals derided him as "Bye Bye Bill." A union insider calling himself Delia Delegate observed in *Crikey*: "His flag is barely still flying, riddled with bullet-holes and mud and blood. His friends say he regrets ever running for President, suspecting that his over-reaching may have triggered the whole split of the Right."

In Canberra, which for Victorian purposes might be called the outside world, Beazley had been toppled after his crushing defeat in the *Tampa* election. Simon Crean failed to inspire excitement as leader of the Opposition. In December 2003, Shorten backed the transition to Mark Latham. His support inspired no affection in the new man. "When I first became leader, Ludwig and Little Billy Shorten pledged AWU support for me,"

Latham wrote in his diary six months later. "But you can't trust them as far as you can kick them." Nevertheless, Latham was guest of honour at the 2004 annual AWU shindig at Crown Casino and sat on Shorten's left. Latham was surprised to find the union leader urging him to support the free trade agreement being negotiated by the Howard government:

> I said that I thought both he and his union were against it, to which he responded, "That's just for the members. We need to say that sort of thing when they reckon their jobs are under threat. I want it to go through. The US Alliance is too important to do otherwise. Politically, you have no choice." Great, the two faces of Little Billy Shorten: Public Shorten against the FTA, Private Billy in favour of it. Is this why he's being groomed for one of the top slots in the corporation? Political courage is not his long suit. Not a bad night otherwise.

Shorten stood above the ruck. Most weeks found him giving speeches. He was writing opinion pieces calling for the defence of jobs, an educated workforce and protection from the pain of globalisation: "The key challenge of future policy will be to manage change with equity." The triumph of his Press Club debut was a couple of years behind him. How journalists had salivated when they found Richard Pratt, ACI Glass Packaging's Peter Robinson, Smorgon's industrial manager Andrew Ashbridge and a squad of Labor leaders gathered in Canberra to watch the young AWU boss do his stuff that day. His theme was the humanising record of unions in the history of Australia: "Yet the Howard Government sells us as the enemy at the gates." The AWU had polled its own members and he knew the men and women of the union overwhelmingly supported Howard blocking the *Tampa*. That election proved a life lesson for Shorten: he saw the power of wedge politics. At the Press Club a few months later, he called on unions to act as a conservative check on the rank and file. Unions represent 2 million workers and who, he asked, do Labor's branches represent?

There is a problem in the party structures when my wife's football club, Hawthorn, has more members than the ALP in Victoria. Some branches are dominated by the few who can endure the *Survivor*-like test of monthly attendances at suburban branch meetings.

Often, it is the union votes at a state conference that stop extremist ALP branch rank-and-file resolutions from becoming party policy. Unions have proven to be useful at assisting the process of sensible party management. If we were to remove union involvement from preselections, there is no guarantee that small inner-suburban ALP branches will get it right.

After Labor's next beating in October 2004, Shorten published a hard critique of Latham's policies and campaign. It was a bold move. By this time, he had been elected to the party's national executive. Even so, he had no official imprimatur to launch this attack. From one defeat to the next, his message had not changed:

Labor's task now is to move to the centre . . .

Howard has retained his conservative supporters in the Right intelligentsia, while gaining newer supporters in "Middle Australia" through his "dog-whistle" rhetoric about issues such as border security, gay marriage and the US alliance.

By contrast, Labor's support has been increasingly confined to the Left intelligentsia with its post-Whitlam emphasis on progressive policies on the environment, refugees and multiculturalism. The policy priorities of the Left are not wrong, but they have acquired a prominence that is now a barrier to Labor reconnecting with both its blue-collar base and middle Australia. The issues of greatest concern to the Left must become less prominent in Labor campaigning.

Howard understands the power of wedge politics . . .

Labor should reject the suggestion that any connection to trade unions is an electoral liability. The everyday experience of working

> for the economic interests of people in the real economy is a valu-
> able policy anchor …

Latham dismissed this in his diary as "absolute horseshit". A few weeks later, in January 2005, Latham was gone and Shorten took a leading role in restoring Beazley to the party leadership. Kevin Rudd had rushed home from the tsunami-devastated coasts of Asia to find his way to the top blocked by an alliance of the Right factions in Queensland, New South Wales and Victoria. They hadn't been as united in a decade. Rudd was per-suaded to keep out of the way and allowed the old leader to return with maximum grace.

Victoria was again in turmoil, but this time Shorten was riding trium-phantly above the confusion. He had pulled off the greatest factional coup of his career. It had taken time, patience and perseverance, but the impact on Labor would be profound. First, Sword fell. The old leader had made the mistake of surrounding himself with young people of talent and ambition while maintaining an iron grip on the union. His protégés came for him in early 2004. Over lunch in a North Melbourne bistro they told Sword his was "a magnificent achievement," but it was time to go. He did so with great dignity. The man who took his place as Victo-rian secretary of the NUW was an old Young Labor sparring partner of Shorten's, Martin Pakula. Public assurances were given that the NUW's "modernisation alliance" with the Left was there to stay. But Shorten and the hirsute Pakula began to talk. They talked all year. In late November, Pakula brought the NUW back into Labor Unity. They called the new alliance Renewal. The deal was done in writing: a peace treaty between warring unions that restored the old order in Victorian Labor and handed power to the ShortCons. For these faction warriors, this was a career-defining achievement. "The resulting alliance now controls about 56 per cent of the numbers in the state branch," Michael Bachelard wrote in the *Australian*. "But such deals come with a price, and their currency is seats in parliament."

The state conference in May 2005 was as vitriolic as anyone could remember, as the Left confronted the reality of Shorten's pact with Pakula. It was a Christmas tree of preselection deals all the way down to little local councils on the fringes of Melbourne. Six members of federal parliament – three of them Opposition frontbenchers – were to be ousted simultaneously. Shorten was promised Maribyrnong. The scale of the operation and the factional conflict it generated through 2005 had not been seen in Victoria for a generation. In August, Shorten further consolidated his position by persuading hardliner Dean Mighell to take the Electrical Trades Union out of the Socialist Left and deliver him another handful of votes. The two men had dealt with each other before as supporters of the run-through rabble-rouser Craig Johnston. The price demanded by Mighell? One federal seat and two in the Victorian parliament.

"I do think the Labor Party needs to constantly be regenerating its parliamentary bloodline," Shorten told Network Ten's *Meet the Press*. That's undisputed. In the melee that consumed Labor in Victoria for nearly a year, a number of difficult political truths had to be faced. Old parliamentarians don't go easily. They fight. To the defence of their little stretch of leather, they bring all their survival skills. But there has to be turnover. In other parties and other states, change is more orderly. The spoils are divided. But in Labor in Victoria, with its shifting loyalties, the factions on top at any particular moment take all. Winners win big and losers lose big. "There are no worries about broken hearts," says Combet. "You have to be tough to survive and Shorten is tough." Victoria is brutal but a great political school. "It throws up people trained in the art of politics," says Gerry Kitchener, a veteran of Labor politics in the state who became an adviser to Julia Gillard. He is not talking about the development of policy – sadly, that's a separate issue – but drumming in basic skills:

> You cannot get a better grounding anywhere in the world. There's dozens upon dozens of people trained in the mechanics of politics

in this state through the factional system. They know what they're doing: they know about polls, they know how to run campaigns. So you've got this grounding. If you want a professional machine, you can't just snap your fingers and expect people to have all these skills.

And the machine is not entirely blind to talent. It can't be. The factions don't guarantee the best people win seats – far from it – but the machine knows talent is survival. Among the time-servers, the burnt-out hacks and the sons of Labor fathers sorted into the parliaments of the nation, there has to be some talent or the party will never see power. As Melbourne was distracted by the Commonwealth Games in early 2006, a new Labor team of promise was selected for Canberra. The Renewal pact took some knocks. Three of the six designated victims managed to survive – the three scalps that had been promised to Pakula and Mighell. What Shorten was promised, he secured. Shorten emerged triumphant.

Isaacs

Anne Corcoran did not go quietly. No one did in these months. She raged against branch stacking. "What is democratic," she asked the *Age*, "about a whole pile of members who don't know they belong to the party, who are having their subscriptions paid for them, who get dragged in by kombi van to a polling booth, given a bit of paper and told, 'You go in there and mark the paper just exactly like this, and we'll take you home again in a few minutes'? How democratic is that?" She won 56 per cent of the local vote. But that was only the first step of the process. In Victoria, equal weight in a Labor preselection is given to the vote of the party's 100-member Public Office Selection Committee. Between them, Shorten and Mighell had sixty or more of those votes. Corcoran was overwhelmed. The contest went to the barrister Mark Dreyfus QC. He was not a faction warrior but a talent pick who became Attorney-General in Rudd's second government and is now Shadow Attorney-General and Shadow Minister for the Arts.

Corio

"I'm not going to have some snot-nosed apparatchik from the right wing of the Labor Party dictating to my constituency who they will have as member," declared Gavan O'Connor. He was wrong. Richard Marles beat him soundly in the local ballot. In the last stages of the contest, an ex-girlfriend of Marles accused him, Feeney, Andrew Landeryou and an unnamed fourth "amigo" of running a slush fund to pay party memberships in Corio. She swore in a statutory declaration: "Richard Marles explained to me that these people would never join if they had to pay their own fees so it was important that enough money was raised or sourced by him during the year to pay for these fees or else he would lose 'numbers'." All three men denied the allegation. Marles became Minister for Trade in Rudd's second government and is now Shadow Minister for Immigration and Border Protection.

Scullin

Harry Jenkins survived a bizarre challenge from a kid called Nathan Murphy from the Electrical Trades Union. He was a protégé of Mighell with not a single run on the board. Even those who negotiated this deal were reported to be embarrassed. Jenkins of the Socialist Left, who had held this rock-solid Labor seat for nearly twenty years, won 62 per cent of the local vote. Shorten's forces were unable to override the rank-and-file mandate. Jenkins was Speaker under Rudd and Gillard, and retired at the 2013 election.

Bruce

Alan Griffin also survived. He was once considered a Labor star for having defeated Shorten's father-in-law, Julian Beale, in 1996, when the rest of the nation was voting the other way. A decade later he was considered ripe for plucking. But he won the local vote handsomely and survived before the selection committee because of the defection of one unknown right-wing delegate. Griffin had the portfolio of veterans affairs under Rudd, to which was added the portfolio of defence personnel under Gillard.

Hotham

The challenge to Simon Crean shocked Labor. He had been leader of the Opposition a little more than a year earlier. It was too soon. Gillard stood up for him. Beazley's refusal to intervene on behalf of his old adversary lost him friends in caucus. Crean effortlessly outsmarted Martin Pakula on the ground, winning an overwhelming 70 per cent of the local vote. The selection committee rubber-stamped the local verdict. Crean became a hero of the party rank and file across the nation. The win revived his fortunes. He became Minister for Trade under Rudd and Minister for Regional Australia, Regional Development and Local Government under Gillard.

But Pakula was NUW and had to be looked after. He was bright and ambitious, with economics and law degrees under his belt. As a consolation prize, the party gave him a seat in the Victorian upper house. That left an unhappy Sang Nguyen, to whom Labor Unity had promised the upper house seat in return for mustering votes in the Vietnamese community. "I've done everything they requested and made no mistakes," he told Michael Bachelard of the *Australian*. "Martin lost his preselection in Hotham, that is his fault, not my fault. Now I have to pay the price." He was particularly furious with Shorten, having, he said, done so much to secure the man's preselection. "There are 70 Vietnamese members in Maribyrnong. I campaigned hard for him. I went doorknocking with him, went to Vietnamese houses with him." Labor's national executive confirmed the discarding of Nguyen. Pakula is now Attorney-General of Victoria.

Maribyrnong

At the seventh annual AWU ball at Crown Casino in October 2005, Bob Hawke led the 1200-strong crowd in all four verses of the old union anthem "Solidarity Forever":

> Is there aught we hold in common with the greedy parasite,
> Who would lash us into serfdom and would crush us with his might?
> Is there anything left to us but to organise and fight?
> For the union makes us strong.

The great of the party had been gathered by Shorten to endorse his push on Canberra. Beazley declared it a privilege to share the platform with "one of our thinkers" and "a terrific union leader in the Bob Hawke tradition." Conroy, Wayne Swan, Craig Emerson and old Bill Ludwig were there. Absent were Kevin Rudd and the sitting member for Maribyrnong, Bob Sercombe. He told the papers he was still waiting for his invitation.

Sercombe had known Shorten was after him for years and had done all he could to shore up his position in this solid Labor stretch of Melbourne that runs south and west of Tullamarine and Essendon airports. For half a dozen years Shorten had been a busy presence in one of the branches in Moonee Ponds. Shorten saw this as doing the chores of a keen member of the party. Sercombe reckoned he was on the prowl. It was a strategic mistake by the old man to abandon the ShortCons in 2002 and go with Sword's Modernisation Alliance. Yet it won him friends at the time. *Crikey* reported that Sword's backers, who hitherto thought Sercombe "a branch-stacking oaf," now called him "a magnificent builder of relationships with ethnic communities, encouraging them to participate in the democratic process." But when Sword fell, Sercombe was left exposed in the selection committee, though regarded as almost unbeatable on the ground. He had increased Labor's lead over the Liberals to nearly 10,000 at the 2004 election. Maribyrnong was known in the party as "Fortress Bob."

But in late 2005, Shorten came to terms with one of the dark legends of the Victorian party, George Seitz, who had been stacking in Maribyrnong for twenty years. No scandal had ever budged Seitz. His energy was endless and so was the money he had on hand to pay party memberships. The Serbian-born Seitz was both state member for Keilor and a power in the Brimbank City Council. Both lay across the map of Maribyrnong. His elite troops were the mainly Macedonian members of the local Sydenham Park Soccer Club, which carries on its clubhouse wall the mission statement "To continually promote all that is righteous in the name of football." Seitz would claim on his deathbed in 2015 that he was persuaded to switch allegiance from Sercombe to Shorten because of the young man's great prospects: "He is the next prime minister, or I hope. That is the basis upon which I supported him." Shorten also tied up Vietnamese votes through Sang Nguyen and Turkish votes through Seitz's detested local rival Hakki Suleyman. The Shorten campaign in Maribyrnong would be all the more colourful for the street brawls that broke out between the Seitz and Suleyman forces. But both were working for him. It was yet another of the unlikely alliances which have advanced his career. Before the formalities of the preselection were complete, he was able to save Seitz from forced retirement. He was sixty-four and the premier had decreed that all Labor MPs in the state must retire at sixty-five. Shorten chaired a meeting of the administrative committee of the party in early 2006 that exempted Seitz from Bracks' decree. Seitz would go on stacking branches until his retirement in 2010.

Sercombe did not go gently. Offers were made and refused. Shorten was polite. He acknowledged the man's long service but argued it was time for change: "We haven't won a federal election since 1993. When your footy team loses four consecutive grand finals, you renew the team." Less elegant were the efforts of his old mate Andrew Landeryou, who pummelled Sercombe week after week in his scandal blog *The Other Cheek*:

> The OC notes that Carmen Sercombe is in fact a very pleasant person, in contrast to the stream of shonks, two-bit crooks, Chinese deal-makers, spooks, sleaze-balls, muck-rakers, branch-stackers, fixers, and scumbags populating the office of Bob Sercombe. I don't know anyone in the ALP who has an unkind word to say about her. But don't start them on Bob.

Landeryou was correspondingly kind to Shorten: "Sercs made an important contribution once, now his sole role in life is blocking a future leader of the ALP from getting preselected. It's a sad way for it all to end."

Shorten knocked on hundreds of doors. He coyly brushed off talk of his ambition. To the people of Sunshine and Essendon, Moonee Ponds and St Albans, he sent a letter of commendation from a remarkable tag team of backers: not only Beazley, Bracks, Hawke, Premier of Queensland Peter Beattie, Bill Ludwig, the New South Wales Right's Mark Arbib and ACTU president Sharan Burrow, but also his old school friend and executive director of the conservative Institute of Public Affairs, John Roskam, and one of the nation's most successful businessmen. "He's hard-working," said Richard Pratt. "He has vision, he's a good communicator and he is interested in the wellbeing of people."

After all that, he won only a narrow victory in the streets of Maribyrnong. Sercombe, with nearly half the local vote, did not see himself as out of the preselection race. He believed his friend Mighell would use his votes on the selection committee to save him. "The old saying about a trade unionist's handshake being his bond applies, especially as Dean says he is about traditional Labor values," said Sercombe. But he was talking about another party at another time. Mighell had done a deal with Shorten. When it was clear he had been deserted, Sercombe withdrew from the race and didn't hold back. He told ABC Radio: "The central problem in the Victorian branch over recent years is they've got an extremely arrogant, very feral Right seeking to throw their muscle round and take everything in their wake." He lashed Shorten: "He's not the messiah, he's just a naughty right-wing boy."

The old Female Orphan School on the campus of the University of Western Sydney is a shrine to Gough and Margaret Whitlam. There's a gallery upstairs named after her and the shop stocks "It's Time" t-shirts. Gathered downstairs in a room that may once have been a dormitory for desperate children are forty university students come to listen to the leader of the Opposition. "What I'm interested in doing is engaging," he tells them. "By engaging, I mean listening. I want to hear your point of view." There are television cameras in the room and a posse of journalists. Breaking all round him that week is news of the deals he had done with Cleanevent and Winslow Constructions all those years ago at the AWU. This would be addressed in a news conference in the courtyard afterwards. With the students he's talking university fees, computer coding, the republic and the damage done to him by so many years of plane travel: "Doctors say I have flight attendant ears."

It's a curious performance: chatty and partisan. He's beating up on the Abbott government and laying on the charm. It's odd to watch the man who would be prime minister trying so hard to be their pal. He takes questions three or four at a time. It's a new technique to let politicians riff freely across half a dozen topics without answering anything in particular. He's not entirely evasive. He's blunt about refugees. Once or twice he earns points by admitting he hasn't an answer: "That's a work in progress." It's hard to gauge the students' mood but they seem pleased to be in Shorten's presence – not remotely awed, but pleased. He is easier to read. He stands before them with his hands in his pockets and a look on his face that says: love me.

So much has been written about this man since he became chief of the AWU fifteen years ago. That's when the newspaper profiles began. There is, for such a brief career, a hefty pile of them. Every profile addresses Shorten's profound self-belief. Every interview about his childhood and university years turns up fresh evidence of his precocious determination to be prime minster. His confidence in himself only grew with time. It irks his colleagues. "He's a capable guy," John Button once remarked on ABC Radio. "In fact, he's mentioned that to me himself several times." His will to power makes sense of his career. As a former Gillard minister told me: "He wants to be PM because he wants to be PM. Everything is about him becoming PM." That takes more than self-belief. Shorten is a serious candidate because he is also willing to lead the life it takes to reach the top: a life hostage at every point to public scrutiny, luck and the intrigue of his colleagues.

But there's a subplot here: his hunger for public affection. Margaret Simons spotted it early in a fine profile written a decade ago as Shorten was manoeuvring to win Maribyrnong:

> Bill Shorten likes to be liked, and he is good at it too. He is handsome, smart, boyishly charming and a reflex flatterer. He is almost a flirt. His weakness, say those who know him, is that he needs to bask in the glow of others' love and admiration. He needs to be loved.

Most politicians do. It's magazine Freud: turning to the public to fill the void. Shorten works at love. He is good with people. He has to an astonishing degree a politician's knack for remembering names and the stories of strangers' lives. He connects. His best work is done face to face. Men and women senior in the party talk of him making contact years ago when they were no more than budding talents. He began bringing them in even then, building his base, recruiting. But in the rough and tumble of the party, his pursuit of affection can seem a little desperate. "It really drives him nuts when someone doesn't like him," a leading adversary in the faction wars told me. "He has to be loved. Even when he fucks you over he wants you to like him – he rings and tries to make up."

Shorten doesn't thrive on hostility. He isn't another Bob Hawke. It's hard to imagine him staring down the unions to open the Australian economy to the world. It's hard to see him trying to persuade Australia to change its mind on any great issue. He works with what's there. By temperament and political disposition he is a numbers man. Shorten isn't built to stand up to panic in the name of principle. A fundamental political lesson of his career was the great wedge of 2001, when Howard took Australia with him by stopping the *Tampa*. Beazley had briefly allowed himself to be wedged. Shorten is determined to avoid that fate. It isn't true he stands for nothing. There's a list of decent, Labor policies he's always backed: jobs, prosperity, education and health. What's counted against him is that he stands for nothing brave.

A student asks: what will Labor do about plans to strip Australians of their citizenship? Shorten won't pledge to block them. He promises merely to be "consistent and constructive." He boasts of Labor's fine-tuning of Abbott's many security laws: "We have made plenty of changes and the government has accepted them." He's asked about refugees and his answer includes the detail that "Richard Pratt was a four-year-old refugee who fled Poland." Would they have a clue who that was? Could they work out where Shorten stands in all this? He's so fuzzy. With great charm he thanks them for their "outstanding questions and a couple of policy suggestions" and departs with the cameras, the press and the acting vice-chancellor in tow.

By the time the Beaconsfield mine disaster was done and dusted, the papers were baying for Shorten to move straight to the Lodge. A few days after Brant Webb and Todd Russell were pulled alive from their rock tomb, Sydney's *Daily Telegraph* splashed across page one: "Bill for PM. Odds Shorten on next Labor leader." Talking for a fortnight at a pithead in northern Tasmania turned Shorten into a national figure. He'd flown home when there seemed no hope of survivors, but when two men were discovered to be alive down there he borrowed Richard Pratt's jet to fly back – just in time, his detractors said, for the Seven Network's *Sunrise*. The town was a mess of miners, press crews and rescue teams. Everything he had learnt at Longford he applied in spades at Beaconsfield. The miners told him what was going on below ground and he told the press. They were hungry for stories. He fed them. There were quotable quotes: drilling through Beaconsfield quartz was like "throwing a Kleenex at rock." Richard Carleton of *60 Minutes* asked the mine manager the tough question: why was it, after an earlier rock fall at the spot where the miners were trapped, "that you continue to send men in to work in such a dangerous environment?" He was then felled on the spot by a heart attack. Shorten wasn't asking any tough questions. He promised those later. "We cannot afford," he said, "to distract from the issue of rescuing the men." Bob Ellis rhapsodised:

> He gave, too, and everybody noticed it, new credibility to the union movement and he did it knowingly. He played the matchless boon of those nine days of media attention like a trusty old harmonica and turned round the popular view of unions as gangs of rorting thugs to decent, conscienceful guardians of Middle Australia, and their safety and their work conditions ... He had clarity, dander, humour, class feeling, momentum, a massive IQ and scads of ambition. He was like Bob Hawke in, say, 1978: on a roll.

But there would be no sudden assumption to Canberra. In May 2006, a fortnight after Beaconsfield, an ACNielsen poll took the wind out of his sails: a mere 9 per cent of those surveyed thought him the best person to lead the country. He came in a distant fourth behind Julia Gillard with 28 per cent, Kevin Rudd with 26 per cent and the struggling Kim Beazley with 21 per cent. And in any case, Bob Sercombe was determined to remain the member for Maribyrnong as long as he possibly could. He invited anyone gullible enough to think he might resign early "to ring me so I can sell them the Sydney Harbour Bridge."

Shorten cleared the decks a little. He handed Cesar Melhem the state secretary's post but remained national boss of the AWU and as busy a factional player as ever in the party. There were still deals to be done. In December, he joined the union bosses who failed to save Beazley in the showdown that brought Kevin Rudd to the leadership. Twice now, Shorten had voted against Rudd. He and the new man would not be natural allies.

Shorten threw himself into the coming election campaign as if every dollar counted. "Maribyrnong was what people would call a safe seat," he told the Royal Commission. "But I was a new candidate and I was committed to my constituents in Maribyrnong, to make sure that I took the campaign seriously." As AWU boss he had dispensed money to election candidates for years: a few hundred dollars here, a few thousand there. Now the money was flowing to him. The Pratts' mansion, Raheen, was the setting for extravagantly successful fundraisers. The union was backing Shorten's campaign. "The AWU was on full campaign mode across Australia," he told the Royal Commission. "We wanted to defeat John Howard and get rid of his WorkChoices laws." And Shorten was turning to the political and business world for the cash he needed to take him to Canberra.

Brian Burke had seen tough times since he turned up to Shorten's Young Labor shindigs in Melbourne. Reports appeared early in the Maribyrnong campaign that the ex-jailbird and former Labor premier of Western Australia had "re-emerged as an influential player and advises

Mr Shorten behind the scenes." In fact, they had been working together for years. Shorten loved Burke. Sometime in the decade after the once-popular politician emerged from prison, Shorten employed him to make peace with union rivals in Western Australia. "Unions can waste a lot of time on demarcation disputes," Shorten explained. "Burke helped us build a relationship with the CFMEU and Kevin Reynolds." Later, Burke helped beat off a challenge to the local AWU leadership. He was riding high again and his lobbying business was flourishing. He held big fund-raising bashes for Labor politicians at Perugino restaurant in Perth, including one for Rudd and another for Shorten. But in late 2006, Burke became a pariah once again when the Corruption and Crime Commission of Western Australia revealed him establishing a covert channel of communication to a minister in the state government. John Howard pounced on Labor's links to Burke. Rudd was fearfully embarrassed. Shorten almost escaped unscathed until Laura Tingle of the *Financial Review* heard a whisper about the Shorten fundraiser. She rang the ALP head office. Seven hours later, Shorten rang to say he had paid the $20,000 back. Next day Tingle reported: "Mr Shorten said he had realised only late last week that cheques had come in to his office, and he had told the ALP's national office yesterday of the funds raised."

In late 2006, Shorten asked Ted Lockyer of Unibuilt, "Ted, would you be willing to employ someone to support my campaign for parliament?" Lockyer was "a bit of a larger-than-life character" who had been dealing with the AWU for a decade or more. He said he was good for $50,000. Shorten had in mind for the job a Young Labor apparatchik called Lance Wilson, who seemed "a good cut of a fellow, young and new." He took Lockyer to a coffee shop round the corner from the union's headquarters in North Melbourne to meet Unibuilt's new employee. Wilson set up a campaign office for the contender in Moonee Ponds and the Unibuilt money began to flow in February 2007.

Several aspects of this arrangement intrigued the Royal Commission. Sometime before polling day, the union and Unibuilt, a labour hire firm, had to negotiate a fresh EBA. Shorten insisted the gift to his campaign didn't hurt the prospects of his members. Unibuilt expected no favours in return:

> The idea that somehow having a discussion with an employer on two different topics, even if not at the same time, and somehow that it is untoward to raise money for election campaigns and do anything else, to me ... that assumes that whenever there is a donation in our electoral system, by anyone, that all other relationships and transactions must immediately be cast into doubt. That is not right, and that is not how I operated at the union.

The paperwork issued by the union falsely stated that Wilson was to be employed by Unibuilt as a researcher. Quite wrong, agreed Shorten: "He was a campaign resource, a campaign director for me." He had asked for the paperwork to be drafted but he can't remember having read it. Again and again, he told Jeremy Stoljar that he left details to his underlings: "When you're the candidate, you don't do all of the paperwork. Your job is to talk to people, be out there."

The deal began to collapse. When the labour hire company proved slow to pay, Wilson was transferred to the AWU payroll and Unibuilt was invoiced $6000 a month. The invoices were also false: they had Wilson working for the AWU rather than Shorten. So how, asked Stoljar, could an auditor tell what the payments were actually for? "You will have to ask the auditor," replied Shorten. And how could the members of the AWU tell from the records? "At the National Executive of the Union there were frequent discussions about how to deal with the WorkChoices laws and the importance of political action against the existing WorkChoices laws."

Unibuilt was about to go bust. After giving a little over $40,000, the payments stopped altogether. From there till polling day, the AWU itself met Wilson's wage. But these gifts from the union and the company were not declared to the Australian Electoral Commission – or not until a few days before Shorten's interrogation before the Royal Commission in 2015.

Why? Shorten said he had only in the last few months discovered the omission. But why wait to amend the declaration until he knew the issue would be raised at the commission? It had taken him and his lawyers till the last minute to find the information, replied Shorten. Politicians of all parties are often guilty of the same failure, he explained. "I can just again say to you: this should have been completely disclosed at the time. I take ultimate responsibility for that."

Shorten's campaign launch in Sunshine featured the Beaconsfield survivors, Russell and Webb, comedian Max Gillies dressed as John Howard, and the Choir of Hard Knocks singing "Love Is in the Air". Shorten was no ordinary candidate. He hit the road from remote Queensland to western Sydney, attacking WorkChoices and selling Labor's policies for jobs, decent hours and fair treatment at work. By this time, the ACTU chief, Greg Combet, had also opted for Canberra, and Howard was on the hustings painting a terrible picture of union domination should Labor be elected. But the public didn't buy it: an *Age*/Nielsen poll shortly before election day, 2007, showed that only a third of those surveyed believed trade unions would "run the country" under Kevin Rudd. Shorten's argument is that union organisers bring more to parliament than Liberal Party apparatchiks. It's an old theme he buffed for his maiden speech:

> On the boards of a woolshed, you know that shearers earn their pay. When you talk to steelworkers at the Port Kembla blast furnaces, to the underground miners at Mount Isa, to the oil workers in Bass Strait in winter or to those who staff the undertakers' night vans as they deal with the grief and tragedy of a road trauma or worse, you know you are in the presence of greatness. When you come face to face with heroism, cooperation and fighting spirit in workplace tragedies such as the Longford gas explosion in Victoria or the Beaconsfield mine collapse in Tasmania, you know you are in the presence of ordinary people performing extraordinary deeds. Every company, every work site I have visited for the last 15 years,

taught me the potential for greatness that individuals carry within them and showed me the limitless capacity of Australian workers and Australian businesses – and, thus, the limitless potential of the Australian economy and Australian society.

Shorten was as safe as houses in Maribyrnong but the post-Beaconsfield euphoria had long evaporated. There was no suggestion now that he would be catapulted to the highest levels of government. Under the old rules he might have muscled his way into cabinet but Rudd had declared that he, not caucus, would decide the ministry. "I will be leading this show," he told the 7.30 Report. "When it comes to the outcomes I want, I will get them." He made Shorten parliamentary secretary for disability services. Shorten had known the old guard would be waiting for him with cricket bats in Canberra, but this was humiliating. A few days earlier he had had a staff of a dozen to run a union 100,000-strong. Now he had five men and women in a distant wing of parliament to pursue the unlikely cause of disability reform. The joke around the building was: "We've fixed Bill up with a job as parliamentary secretary for people who can't wipe their own arses."

He sought advice. Gillard told him it was a chance to show another side of himself. Kelty advised him to put his head down and work. "If you want to be really good, you've got to do an apprenticeship in life. Hawke did that. Howard in his miserable way did it too. So did Keating as treasurer. He worked and worked. You've got to work for this job." He meant the leadership. After an angry few days, Shorten decided the only option was success. "This is going to be a campaign," he promised Kelty. "I will not join the queue of do-gooders."

Labor MPs were puzzled to find that the man whose arrival had been heralded by trumpets took so little part in caucus. He rarely put up his hand. "He just didn't trouble the scorers," said one senior Labor figure. Shorten remained a factional warlord and was highly successful in his portfolios, but was not a party leader. "If you looked objectively at who was doing what on the floor of the parliament, who was doing what in policy reform, contributing in the cabinet, contributing in the caucus, contributing in the ministry, it wasn't Shorten. Not even close. Not even in the top tier. Not even part of the A-team." A measure of his absence from the inner workings of power in Canberra can be gauged from the many memoirs already published from this time. Save for his role in the great executions, Shorten's name barely appears in the indexes. He had a lot to learn. Parliament was something entirely new. He told the *Sunday Age* he was warned it would be hard. "People give you this advice from outside of Parliament, and they say, 'Oh, it's like going to the big school now.' And I thought, 'Oh, yeah, I've been around, done a bit.' But they're right. It is big … I'm amazed at what I didn't know about Parliament until I got there."

*

A month after he walked the Kokoda Track in July 2008, Shorten left his wife. To the end, they were regarded as a power couple. They had no children. IVF had failed. Their big house in Moonee Ponds was empty. Shorten told an old comrade from Young Labor: "It's nothing to do with my sperm." In the last months before coming to Canberra, he had met the daughter of the governor of Queensland. The *Courier-Mail*'s vice-regal column noted in September 2007: "In the evening, the Governor received the call of Ms Chloe Bryce-Parkin and Mr Bill Shorten." No one was reading the tea-leaves. Chloe was formidably glamorous, wife of the resort architect Roger Parkin, a mother of two and spokeswoman for Cement Australia. The Shortens parted in August 2008. It is always reported that he left his first wife abruptly at a football game. He denies this. Many doors in Establishment Melbourne shut in his face. Others opened, for in September his new partner's mother became governor-general. Chloe was pregnant in the winter of 2009 and they married in Melbourne that November: she in white, he in a grey pinstripe suit with a rose in his lapel. This time the ceremony was at St Thomas Anglican Church in Moonee Ponds. To the utter bafflement of his friends, Shorten had become an Anglican.

"I believe in God," he says. "Like a lot of Australians I don't want to talk about my faith, but I'm not an atheist. I think that things happen with the influence of God. My wife wanted us to be married in the Anglican faith and there was a very good priest who supported us. So I thought, fair enough, I'm happy to belong to a church willing to marry two people who are divorced." He hasn't reneged on Catholicism entirely. Pope Francis he thinks impressive: "A remarkable guy. A breath of fresh air." Catholic social teaching is still in his head, along with the "golden rule" every boy was taught at Xavier: "It was at the heart of the Jesuit call to be a 'man for others.' And I have spent my working life, both representing workers and as parliamentarian, trying to measure up to this standard of compassion and empathy." What repels Shorten are "Sunday Christians who wear their religiosity on their sleeves and then lecture people all week. I'm uncomfortable with the view that God has a really strong opinion about who I'm living with. I don't believe that God has a strong view on IVF or stem-cell research." Here he finds Melbourne's relaxed brand of Anglicanism particularly attractive, with its respect for science, acceptance of women priests and attitude to marriage, including gay marriage. With a candour not shown by Rudd or Gillard when they were Labor leaders, Shorten called the Australian Christian Lobby on its vengeful attitudes to sex and marriage. This is personal for him:

> When I hear people invoking the scriptures to attack blended families like mine, I cannot stay silent. I do not agree. When I see people hiding behind the Bible to insult and demonise people based on who they love, I cannot stay silent. I do not agree. When I hear people allege that "God tells them'" that marriage equality is the first step on the road to polygamy and bigamy and bestiality, I cannot stay silent. I do not agree. These prejudices do not reflect the Christian values I believe in ... I believe in God and I believe in marriage equality under the civil law of the Commonwealth of Australia.

War had broken out again in Victoria. Hostilities began with the Short-Cons trying to pay their debts to the Turkish stackers in Maribyrnong. They were owed the preselection of Natalie Suleyman for the state seat of Kororoit. When this was blocked by rival George Seitz, the Right began to tear itself apart. Things came to a head after six months with an attempt to knock off the state secretary of the party, Stephen Newnham. Premier John Brumby put his own job on the line to beat back the challenge. A few weeks later, Shorten regained his grip on the party with a daring manoeuvre: he took the ShortCons out of Labor Unity and into a pact with former teacher Kim Carr, the lion of the Socialist Left. Together they could carve up the seats between them. Feeney was betrayed and Labor Unity reduced to a rump. Once again, a splendid name was found for this pragmatic bastardry: the Stability Pact. "It is a bit tough," remarked one of the now powerless faction leaders, "to describe Pearl Harbor as a stability agreement." For six months the pact was assailed by the far Right and far Left, until a fresh peace was struck between Shorten and Feeney in June 2009. Stability Pact II delivered yet more votes to Shorten in the councils of the party in Victoria. Along the way, a successor was found for Newnham. The deal was done by telephone hook-up out of the deputy prime minister's office. Gillard's adviser Gerry Kitchener recalls: "Parliament was sitting – it turns out that the next day Conroy was introducing the NBN legislation – and there's Gillard, Feeney, Conroy, Shorten on the phone with Brumby and a couple of his advisors in Gillard's office, locked away for three hours thrashing out a deal on who became State Secretary. It was the ultimate obsession about the factional stuff."

Shorten had taken up the cause of the disabled with passion. Gillard wrote: "He actually fell in love with the policy area and the possibility of making change for so many Australians leading such difficult lives." Care for the disabled in Australia was a long-recognised shambles. Your fate depended not on need, but on how and where you came by your disability. At birth? On a building site? Insured or uninsured? New South Wales or Queensland? Billions were being spent on care but billions more were needed to do the job properly. Out of Rudd's talkfest, the Australia 2020 Summit, came the idea of a national insurance scheme rather like Medicare, with every citizen paying a small levy to meet the costs of disability. This idea was not new but had found an effective advocate in Bruce Bonyhady, a banker who had two sons with cerebral palsy. Shorten knew nothing about disability care. Bonyhady taught him. A few weeks after the summit, Shorten appointed a team of bankers and financiers to investigate the insurance scheme. The hope was that they would find fresh ways of raising the enormous amounts of money required. They had over a year to report, while Shorten brought his AWU experience to the task of welding the disability community into one forceful lobby. He would say: "I wished the sector was as well organised as a trade union." Each group dealing with autism or cerebral palsy or dyslexia railed at governments to meet their individual needs. "That is what has failed spectacularly for decades," Shorten told Laura Tingle. "So what you've got to do is give them a common set of claims." He called what he was doing "a case of classic old-fashioned organising."

Rudd was full of praise for his efforts. After the brutal fires in the hinterland of Melbourne in early 2009, he added bushfire reconstruction to Shorten's responsibilities. But he did not promote him in the reshuffle of June 2009. Combet went into the cabinet ahead of him and so did the NSW Right boss, Mark Arbib. Commentators took it to be a deliberate snub. A few days later, a disconsolate Shorten called on the US consul-general, Mark Thurston, in Melbourne. Thurston sent a note of their meeting to Washington:

> Shorten makes no bones about his ambitions in federal politics. During a June 11 meeting, Shorten told Consul General that "he did not take this job to stand still." He explained that he had been overlooked for promotion in Prime Minister Rudd's June 6 cabinet reshuffle in order to keep the geographical balance in the cabinet between

Victoria and New South Wales. (Comment: Despite words to the contrary, Shorten appeared disappointed while he was discussing this topic. End comment.) ...

Shorten said that he is deeply influenced by Martin Luther King Jr. and quoted from several of his speeches in our meeting with him. While National Secretary of the powerful Australian Workers' Union, he spent time in the United States collaborating with the United Steel Workers' union ... He is widely known for his pro-U.S. stance ...

Bill Shorten is part of a new generation of articulate, young labour union leaders ... He has an MBA from Melbourne University, was close to the late packaging mogul Richard Pratt, and said that in comparison to other union leaders, he is willing to listen to business concerns ...

Shorten, who is somewhat rumpled in appearance, prefers to get down to business quickly in meetings. He is a nimble conversationalist who understands nuance. In addition to being cautious, considered and thoughtful, he is able to skilfully steer away from topics he prefers to avoid ... he admitted that he is still getting his feet wet in Parliament and that things there are "more complicated than he thought." Despite his lukewarm relationship with Prime Minister Rudd (he sided with Kim Beazley in the 2006 ALP leadership ballot), Shorten struck us as highly ambitious but willing to wait — at least for a while — for his moment in the sun.

The Shortens began to appear together as he went about his political chores. Their daughter Clementine was born a few months after their marriage. To Shorten's delight he found himself a father of three: one of his own and two of Chloe's. He told an old friend from his Monash days: "That's what it's all about." Everything was going well in Canberra. Rudd appointed him to his little committee of Left and Right powerbrokers who were supposed to settle preselection disputes across the country. Even so, Shorten was never part of Rudd's circle. Neither Kevin nor Therese warmed to him. Yet there was no doubt the prime minister backed his work on disability reform. When the bankers and financiers endorsed the National Disability Insurance Scheme, Rudd passed the idea to the Productivity Commission. Shorten declared the cause "the last practical frontier of civil rights."

Then Rudd began to fall apart. By early winter 2010 he was distrusted by caucus and loathed by most of his ministers. Plans to tax the bonanza being enjoyed by mining companies in one of the great booms in Australian history rallied enemies inside and outside the party. Elections were due within months. Published polls suggested Labor had a fight on its hands. Private polling commissioned by the party was pointing to heavy losses. In Maribyrnong and on the disability circuit Shorten was listening to voters disgruntled and bemused by the direction Rudd was taking. By June he had formed the view that the government was "in electoral trouble of a very serious nature." He was coming to the conclusion: "We had to do something significant." On the Queen's Birthday weekend he was with Rudd in Western Australia, helping sell the mining tax to miners. Barrie Cassidy reports in *The Party Thieves* that Shorten decided to break with Rudd at a doorstop interview on that trip:

> He was dismayed to hear Rudd talk of how he intended to carve up the infrastructure dividend from the mining tax. Rudd told the media that he would split the money three ways between Western Australia, Queensland and the rest of Australia. Shorten found that a bizarre formula that ran counter to all the principles of federation. He had heard and seen enough. At that moment, he decided that as soon as he returned to the eastern states, he would seek a meeting with Gillard.

A few days later he warned her that Labor might well be wiped out and raised the possibility of her challenging Rudd. He said she "should think about this." Gillard kept her own counsel.

Shorten was not the chief assassin. The idea of sacking the prime minister had been in the air for weeks in Canberra. He was not the first person to urge Gillard to run. The NSW Right minister Tony Burke had raised that with her several times. Unauthorised polling in Victoria was brought to Gillard that showed her approval rating climbing through the roof. The party also polled in four marginal NSW seats, and officials who saw the results on Friday 18 June thought, "We're bloody stuffed." When a by-election next day at the foot of the Blue Mountains saw a 25 per cent swing against Labor, the Right in New South Wales was ready to trigger a caucus spill. On the Monday, the *Australian* carried a most encouraging Newspoll that showed Labor in a winning position, with a two-party-preferred vote of 52 to 48. Rudd was delighted but it didn't give the plotters pause. Shorten wanted Rudd gone but on the night of 22 June he clearly did not know what would happen next. He would say: "It was spontaneous."

A *Sydney Morning Herald* story claiming Rudd was suspicious of Gillard's intentions set the coup in motion. Feeney thought the story the last straw and saw Arbib. Together they went to Gillard's office about 9.30 a.m. She was furious. They urged her to run. The Right of Victoria and New South Wales were already in lock-step, but it was only after this meeting with Gillard that the two faction leaders brought Conroy and Shorten into the loop. From this point, all four men were active players in Rudd's down-fall. Arbib was their leader but Kitchener says: "I honestly don't think she would've moved without Shorten." After Question Time, the four met Gillard in Kim Carr's office for over an hour. For connoisseurs of faction play, it was a notable gathering of old enemies and fresh allies brought together in the Stability Pact. But it was not without strain. At some point in this remarkable day, Feeney is said to have told Shorten: "Don't mistake this for unity on the Victorian Right." Gillard went to see Rudd. While that meeting continued, Shorten and a group of plotters went to the Hoang Hau restaurant in Kingston. Cameras followed them. Shorten was filmed making many calls on his mobile phone. He insists he was not rallying the numbers but talking to his step-daughter's teacher. Right or wrong, what the cameras saw that night became what Shorten calls the "infamous footage" of the plot against Rudd.

Gillard was with Rudd for two hours. They came to a strange arrangement: Rudd would step down if, closer to the time, it was felt he was an impediment to Labor's re-election. Senator John Faulkner would act as umpire. Gillard went to an anteroom in the prime minister's suite and rang Conroy. He told her it was too late. Caucus had already made up its mind. She went back to Rudd. "I am now advised that you no longer have the confidence of the caucus," she said. "I am therefore requesting a leadership ballot." She returned to her own office, which soon filled with MPs. They were crunching her numbers. Kitchener would tell the ABC television series *The Killing Season*:

> Shorten was in the office, he was down the back, but he throughout the evening was bringing MPs – a lot of MPs from Queensland – to meet with Julia. I think it's fair to say that whatever Bill's faults may or may not be, he knows how to work the numbers and he was bringing people until late in the night.

Everyone else had stopped but Shorten kept going. "He was still dragging people in at 1.30 in the morning when Gillard was leaving to go home," says Kitchener. "It was all over Red Rover and he chased down every single vote possible." Later, in the corridors, Kitchener bumped into Arbib, who, never one to miss an opportunity, pulled out a wish-list for Gillard's first ministry. He came to Shorten's name. Kitchener told the ABC:

> He said you couldn't trust Bill Shorten, that he would do Julia in, that the one thing she couldn't do was ever give him industrial relations, because he would use it to solidify the union base to knock her off.

She would do that, and he did that, but Arbib claims Kitchener's account of his warning is rubbish. On the far side of a difficult election campaign in August, which Gillard barely survived, Shorten was called to Yarralumla to be sworn in by his mother-in-law as Assistant Treasurer and Minister for Financial Services and Superannuation. He still had no seat at the cabinet table.

This man is a magnet for nicknames. True, there is rich material in Bill and Shorten. Anyone would be tempted. Growing up with a surname like that wouldn't be easy in any playground. But for most of his forty-eight years Shorten has *inspired* nicknames. They're part of his story. Here's a culled list:

Monash University
I Finally Won Something Shorten — *Lot's Wife*, 1987
Bill "Career-Move" Shorten — *Lot's Wife*, 1987

AWU
Golden Boy — his staff, 2001
Bye Bye Bill — factional opponents, 2002
King Billy — workers, Nonferral Pty Ltd, 2005
Showbag Shorten — AWU, by 2005
The ET of Spring Street — Bob Sercombe, ousted Member for Maribyr-
nong, 2005
Little Billy Shorten — Mark Latham, 2005
Braveheart — factional foes, 2006

Government
Bill the Knife — various, July 2013

Opposition
Electricity Bill — Tony Abbott, October 2013
The Prince of Darkness — Kathy Jackson, 2014
Adora-Bill — his staff, early 2014
Mr Potato Head — Christopher Pyne, March 2014
Bull Shittin — Derryn Hinch, April 2014
Barnacle Bill — Tony Abbott, November 2014

From this distance, it may seem Gillard's ministers did nothing for three years but plot. Yet a good deal of work was done. Shorten attacked the task of patching up the superannuation system with the energy, if not the passion, he had brought to caring for the disabled. He set about mastering the complications of a system that had produced the fourth biggest pool of retirement funds in the world and an industry that guarded its immense profits with trip-wires and mastiffs. He was embarking on another of the primal battles with money fought by the Rudd and Gillard governments. They lost to miners, Murdoch and poker machines. Shorten pulled off a draw with the superannuation industry.

He worked well with Gillard. They were old factional allies long before the ShortCons forced her hand the night of Rudd's defenestration. Despite the Left label she had worn since her university days, Gillard's career depended on the Right. They gave her Lalor in 1998 on the strength of talent alone. After that she voted with the Right and they controlled the numbers in her seat. She had her own tiny subfaction known as the Ferguson Left, but her base in Victoria was broad and at its heart were the ShortCons. She was a party to the Stability Pact. Between the new prime minister and her junior minister for superannuation, there was no factional tension. Nor was he ever a contender for her job. Shorten had spent only three winters in Canberra. Everyone knew his ambitions were huge, but as the Gillard government set to work it seemed that his time, if it were to come, was a long way off. She appointed him to the Expenditure Review Committee. He was not tough. "She wasn't one to bag people, but you knew when she didn't like or respect people," says her adviser Gerry Kitchener. "I think she respected him and I think she respected his talents." But there were ministers who sensed she didn't trust him.

Shorten knew about superannuation. Like many senior union officials, he had been director of an industry fund: in his case, Australian Super, with $30 billion under management. Commercial super funds bleated at times that the new minister had an innate conflict of interest. He stared them down. Shorten fought significant battles on two fronts: one was to compel financial advisers to act in the best interests of their clients, and the other was to provide a standard, simple, low-cost default fund called MySuper, into which everyone's money would be paid unless other arrangements were made. Both ideas had been recommended by several inquiries into the finance industry. Both were fought hard. The behemoth Keating and Hawke had created was more than willing to use its immense resources to oppose change. The independent MP Rob Oakeshott remembers the scene as Shorten began work: "The five peak bodies, pushing competing positions, not only set up camp in the corridors of parliament to give advice, but bombarded electorate offices around Australia with their views."

Shorten's notices were good as he took on the industry in public and private. "This week the apprentice outshone the master," declared the *Australian* in December 2010. "Bill Shorten selling superannuation reforms left Wayne Swan looking second-rate as he struggled to sell his banking measures." What followed was a year's intense advocacy and negotiation. There were complaints that the new minister was not a master of the minutiae as the old minister, Chris Bowen, had been. But Paul Barry, writing on the Power Index website, saw the gap Shorten was filling in Gillard's team:

> Shorten brings to the role something in limited supply within Labor: a capacity to effectively prosecute a case. For all the criticism of Labor's union links and the structural limitations it places on party reform, the more effective unions continue to produce men and women trained to effectively argue a case publicly.

Some questioned whether the dispute-by-dispute approach of a seasoned union official produced the best result. When Shorten announced the final package of reforms in September 2011, it was declared something of a miracle that he had bridged the chasm between the parties. A version of MySuper had been agreed. Financial advisers were to be made more accountable to their clients than their masters. But the question remained: had Shorten gone too far to placate the retail funds? Everyone was more or less happy, but had he, in union jargon, "settled soft"?

Gillard reshuffled her cabinet in December. Support for her had fallen away and fresh storms were always on the horizon. The loss of a single supporter in the House might doom her government. Polls showed no great confidence she would be prime minister in a year's time. The reshuffle revealed how difficult her position was within the party. No great changes were made. Some ministers simply refused to budge. Shorten's promotion to cabinet as Minister for Employment and Workplace Relations was one of the few changes that was plainly on merit. Shorten had campaigned for the job. In the Qantas dispute that led to the grounding of the whole fleet in October, he had outshone the minister he was replacing. The press reported every move. It was a sign of his growing strength that Gillard allowed him to keep responsibility for superannuation while taking on industrial relations. While this brought him into the inner cabinet, it did not hand him any heavy reform agenda. Gillard had seen off Howard's hated WorkChoices, and while radical unions and big industry complained about the new *Fair Work Act*, Shorten's task was mainly to tinker and supervise. He came into the job making his old boast that he could work both sides of the aisle: "I don't believe it's too difficult to be pro-employer and pro-employee at the same time." Laura Tingle in the *Financial Review* called the new minister "the union fox in the industrial relations chook shed."

Shorten had no doubt where his loyalties lay when Rudd came for Gillard weeks after the reshuffle. Rudd had been briefing journalists and whispering in caucus for months, but only broke cover when an embarrassing little clip was posted on YouTube. "This fucking language," he shouts, banging the table in frustration. "How can anyone do this?" These were out-takes of the foreign minister recording a video greeting in Mandarin. He is beside himself with rage. "Tell them to cancel this meeting at six o'clock. I haven't the fucking patience to go." With this humiliating clip on the net, Rudd offered himself to Sky; blamed Gillard's office for his embarrassment; and flew to Washington. Shorten might have stayed in the background, but found himself a few nights later on *Q&A*, where he denied rumours he was negotiating to be treasurer under a resurrected Rudd.

> I support the Prime Minister, for the same reasons that I supported her in June of 2010 and now. She is the best person for the job. She is the person who's strong. She's getting on with business … She's had to negotiate legislation through a hung parliament, a minority government, and what she's managed to do is quite remarkable.

Finally Gillard and key ministers let Australia know what life with Kevin PM had been like. Shorten did not join this outpouring of scorn. He did not, as Nicola Roxon did, declare he would never serve under the man. Labor's candour did not sway Australia. Even as party leaders were dumping on Rudd, pollsters were told a switch to him would crush Abbott. Shorten and Conroy did the numbers for the prime minister in caucus. The AWU block of 15 was solid. The entire union movement was backing her. When the vote came in late February 2012, she won by 71 votes to 31. Rudd promised never to challenge her again. He didn't pause.

It was a tainted year. In May, Shorten and his wife had to parade themselves in the *Herald Sun* under the headline "Our Love is Strong" to deny unspecified rumours – freely available on the net – of his infidelity. "Life's a journey of experiences," he told the paper. "I am in a good place right now and at the centre of that is the kids and Chloe." Labor accused the Opposition of spreading the gossip. Joe Hockey blamed the unions. Meanwhile, Peter Slipper had been ambushed with accusations – never proved – of sexual harassment. Opposition politicians were deeply involved in this attack on one of their own, a Liberal who had defected to become Speaker and thus shore up Gillard's government. The question was: could he continue in the role while civil action was pending against him? "These matters are for Mr Slipper to consider," Shorten declared. "I'm sure he's actually considering the question you asked very carefully." Gillard had other ideas: she needed Slipper where he was. There followed a famous exchange between Shorten and Sky's David Speers:

SPEERS: Do you think he should return to the Speaker's chair while the civil claims are still being played out?

SHORTEN: I understand the Prime Minister's addressed this in a press conference in Turkey in the last few hours. I haven't seen what she said, but let me say I support what it is that she's said.

SPEERS: Hang on. You haven't seen what she said ...

SHORTEN: But I support what my Prime Minister's said.

SPEERS: Well, what's your view?

SHORTEN: My view is what the Prime Minister's view is.

The comedy was undeniable. From distant London, the *Guardian* asked: "Is Bill Shorten the world's most loyal politician?" But veteran Canberra commentator Michelle Grattan saw the exchange rather differently: "Shorten was clearly distancing himself." Reports of the Slipper imbroglio were peppered with speculation that Shorten was positioning himself to challenge a crippled Gillard for the leadership. This was pure mischief. Poll after poll showed support for him taking her job didn't run into double figures.

Scandal followed scandal. Only days after the Slipper story broke, Shorten took the brawling Health Services Union to the Federal Court. Again, Gillard's survival was on the line, for at the heart of this sordid narrative was the member for Dobell and former general secretary of the union, Craig Thomson. Labor had protected him for as long as it could. The party had even contributed to his legal costs when he tried and failed to sue the Fairfax press over stories about him using his union credit card to buy sex. The end of the line was the report of an investigation into the union by Fair Work Australia that landed on Shorten's desk in early April. Thomson was cut loose from the Labor Party and sent to the crossbenches. Before releasing the 1000-page exposure of his corruption, Shorten announced the government would swiftly legislate to improve the financial oversight of unions, increase penalties and speed up investigations.

The report revealed a fortune wasted on opulent living, prostitutes and funding Thomson's path to Canberra. The union had spent over $250,000 on his election alone. Shorten's response was to force the combined NSW, ACT and Victorian branches of the union into administration. Action of this kind in the Federal Court had never been taken before. It earned him the ire of a very old political friend, the new national secretary of the union, Kathy Jackson. She called his move "a cheap political stunt." She too would be brought down in this squalid saga, but not before she inflicted some carefully calibrated damage on Shorten.

In an affidavit she couldn't persuade the court to accept, Jackson gave a spirited account of a confrontation with Shorten, one he denies ever took place. The scene was the party's Melbourne headquarters and the occasion a preselection contest for the marginal seat of Corangamite. According to the affidavit, Jackson had gone out for a cigarette when Shorten approached and asked her to back his candidate, Peter McMullin. Jackson says she refused:

JACKSON: I can't vote for him.

SHORTEN: Why not.

JACKSON: Because he is part of Spotless. Spotless have been screwing our outsourced members. I cannot vote for someone who is associated with a business that is screwing our members.

Jackson says the veins were showing in his forehead. "He said words loudly to the effect: 'You will fucking well vote for the candidate that I tell you to vote for. If you defy me, you will never be welcome in my home again and you will never have our support when you fucking well need it.'" McMullin wasn't preselected. Shorten threatened to sue the *Financial Review* if the story appeared. It was published in late June.

As if that were not enough filth to contend with, the sacked attorney-general, Robert McClelland, chose this moment to accuse his party of being soft on union corruption. "I know the Prime Minister is quite familiar with this area of the law," he said. "As lawyers in the mid-1990s, [we] were involved in a matter representing opposing clients." He was pointing to the old AWU scandals involving Gillard's then-partner Bruce Wilson. McClelland had been employed back then to try to claw money back from Wilson. The media took up the issue with renewed relish. Gillard repeated her old denials. Gun journalist at the *Australian* Hedley Thomas got to work, and a river of stories began flowing through the paper, seeking to tie Gillard to Wilson's frauds. Shorten did not back Gillard all the way. He condemned the slush fund she had set up for her boyfriend. "That account was unauthorised by the union," he told *Lateline*. "It was an inappropriate account. That account, as far as I can tell, was out of bounds." Thomas and his team wrote over 80,000 words, produced remarkable documents, showed young Gillard to have been a sloppy lawyer, failed to implicate her in any crimes but did the prime minister untold damage.

Rudd was circling all the time. The polls, which seemed to be turning in Gillard's favour towards the end of 2012, fell away in the New Year. Shorten backed Gillard unequivocally at the AWU conference in February 2013 but more loudly than ever he was being urged by the commentariat to abandon her. The flattery of Rudd's people came with threats: be kingmaker now or never be king. Success had turned Shorten into a trophy. So had his endless promotion in the press as the leader down the track. He had come to represent legitimacy within the party. The faceless man of 2010 was the lieutenant both Gillard and Rudd wanted seen by their side. The contest between these rivals could be analysed as a battle between old Labor and new; between a party of unions and a party of civilians. But the contest was really more personal, simpler and infinitely sad. This was a battle between a man who couldn't do the job and a woman who could; between a charismatic exile and a leader deserted by the public; between a saboteur who might win and an incumbent who seemed not to have a hope.

Rudd made another fumbling attempt in March 2013. Shorten was conspicuously at Gillard's side throughout the bizarre day when Rudd, in the end, flinched from the contest. "It's been a big and eventful day," said Shorten in the aftermath. "We've got a strong leader that's unanimously endorsed by her team and I think the end of the day speaks for itself." But the meaning of the day was slow to unfold. One sign was the defection of Richard Marles to Rudd. The ShortCons were not holding fast. Under the extreme stress of the contest, the discipline of the factions was breaking down. It didn't help that despite the great events in Canberra, the Right in Victoria was feuding for the usual reason: a safe seat was on the market. Nicola Roxon was leaving politics and wanted a former staffer, Katie Hall, to have Gellibrand. Conroy wanted it for his staffer, Tim Watts. A third contender was Kimberley Kitching, a one-time Melbourne city councillor who had been hired to clean up the HSU mess in Victoria. There was a strong Shorten connection: Kitching was married to his old friend, the blogger Andrew Landeryou. But the women pulled out. Watts got the seat.

Cabinet did a good deal of soul-searching after Rudd's second challenge. Shorten was still not a big presence at the table. His focus remained on his portfolios and the factional hinterland. His superannuation reforms had become law in 2012, and in early 2013 Jenny Macklin shepherded the National Disability Insurance Scheme through parliament. These were big achievements for which he could take a great deal of credit. But when he turned his mind in cabinet to the survival of the government, Shorten appeared to have little to contribute. One minister recalls:

> When governments are on the decline there comes a moment when the leader lets it run at cabinet and there's a debate. Now this is a government in trouble and Julia's opened it up for examination and there's some really good analysis from Tony Burke and Craig Emerson. I forget who else contributed. Do you know what Bill says? "Our senators aren't opening their offices in marginal seats. They've got their offices in the CBD." And I thought at the time, does he really believe this is even worth discussing here? You could have

every Labor senator close his office in the central business district and move out to a marginal seat and it wouldn't make the faintest difference to the problems plaguing the Gillard government. It was the best he could come up with. I thought, if this is the guy who's being promoted as a future leader ...

Shorten was changing his mind about Gillard as the numbers flowed towards Rudd. He was deeply troubled. The AWU stood foursquare behind the Prime Minister and so did Conroy. For the first time in his political life, Shorten contemplated breaking with his closest allies. He admired and liked Gillard, but he had seen polling that suggested Labor's numbers in the House of Representatives would be halved if she led them to election day. He paid for a poll in Maribyrnong that showed a 13 per cent swing against him: this Labor prize would become marginal. There was no factional discipline in the drift towards Rudd. Individuals were making up their own minds. In some worlds, that's how politics works. Penny Wong had gone across. Kim Carr was happily behind Rudd again. The NSW Right was behind the contender and threatening to ignore Shorten in future leadership contests if he didn't shift too. Shorten was almost over the line. On Sunday 9 June, Barrie Cassidy set the contest ablaze by declaring on Insiders that Gillard would not be leading Labor to the next election. Swan would blame Shorten for lighting the match. Cassidy denies this. Shorten continued to maintain that he was backing the prime minister: "I support her and continue to support her." He saw Gillard just before the Midwinter Ball and told her how deeply concerned he was. He let her know the writing was on the wall. Convinced he had already switched, her people froze him out of strategic discussions. But Shorten says he vacillated almost until the last day:

> I hoped that this would pass, that somehow she would work it out, or he would work it out, or that they would work it out. Having been through one change I really did not want to be part of another change. No one has ever suggested I undermined Julia. My motivation

seriously about the second change was a lot more thought-out, and a lot more difficult, and with a lot of scar tissue from the first change.

I didn't think that Labor would win more than 25 or 30 seats if we stuck with Julia. I thought we were heading for Armageddon. My logic was that there are millions of people who put their trust in Labor and we had to come up with a better answer.

Shorten and Rudd met in Marles' office during the press gallery's Midwinter Ball on 19 June. Rudd was laying down conditions: he wouldn't save Labor from annihilation unless Shorten publicly backed his putsch. Both men disliked and distrusted each other. "Shorten wanted to hear Rudd make his case; he wanted to know Rudd was committed," Paul Kelly reports in *Triumph and Demise*. "Rudd, on the other hand, needed Shorten to sign up for change. Shorten had become a prize. But Shorten did not pledge to Rudd; he was too cautious, too distrustful." Asked a couple of days later on Melbourne radio by Neil Mitchell if he had discussed the leadership with Rudd, Shorten lied blind.

Gillard called on the contest on 26 June. She was all but certain she had lost the numbers. Shorten rang in the late afternoon to say he would be voting against her. She was not surprised. He only made his position public in the corridor outside the party room: "I have now come to the view that Labor stands the best chance to defend the legacy of this term of Parliament and to continue to improve the lives of millions of Australians with Kevin Rudd as our leader." He added: "I understand that this position that I have adopted may come at a personal cost to myself." He was all but alone. He had no faction behind him. His statement may have given comfort to waverers in caucus, but the head-counters of the party say Shorten brought only one other vote with him into the room. He didn't decide the issue but he was determined to own it. Why not just let it happen? "Because that's not leadership. A lot of other people didn't say what they were doing. But if I ever wanted to be a leader of this party, I didn't have the luxury of hiding."

Dyson Heydon brought only a couple of sheets of paper into the royal commission. His face was set. With dry formality he read a list of applications made, documents delivered and submissions received from half a dozen unions and the ACTU, asking him to stand down from his post. He spoke in the passive. It was as if he were somehow at a huge distance from himself. After five minutes he got to the point: "I have considered all the submissions. In my opinion the applications must be dismissed. I publish my reasons." This was not a loss for Shorten. That the commissioner decided to stay gives Labor a chance to eke out this scandal all the way to the election.

Shorten was still licking his wounds after his own appearance in the box when the news broke in August that Heydon was to give the Sir Garfield Barwick Address to a Liberal Party fundraiser. Every accusation of political bias Labor and the unions had levelled at the commission seemed vindicated. Heydon instantly cancelled the engagement "for sensible reasons of risk management and self-preservation," he said, "to avoid the attacks of the suspicious and the malicious." And they poured down on his ancient head. Parliament was in uproar. Labor was triumphant. Abbott was again on the back foot, defending one of his pet projects. For Shorten, Labor and the unions, it was as if the sun had broken through a thick bank of cloud.

Marcus Priest, a sharp-eyed former journalist and adviser to Labor attorneys-general, had thought the invitation to hear Heydon talk at the Castlereagh Hotel was peculiar: it was covered with advertising for the Liberal Party and came with a form encouraging donations. Priest rang the New South Wales Bar Association; they contacted Stoljar; he had a word to the commissioner next morning; and hours later the Liberal organisers of the dinner learnt that Heydon would not, in fact, be delivering his address on "The Judicial Stature of Chief Justice Barwick Viewed in a Modern Perspective."

Heydon's account of how he got himself into this pickle was so like Shorten's evidence: he hadn't read the documents; matters were left to his staff; he wasn't across the detail; one or two crucial facts had slipped his mind; and no matter how bad things might appear, his integrity remained absolute. Most unlike Shorten was the political naivety of Heydon's 67-page exculpation. He could not be expected to admit that the commission's task was of high importance in some respects but a political stitch-up in others. That would be to admit he should never have taken on the job. But in explaining his decision not to step down, Heydon made bizarre claims: that his was not an inquiry into the Labor Party, and the appearance of a former Labor prime minister and the current Labor leader of the Opposition had nothing to do with politics:

> Ms Gillard ... gave evidence not because she wanted to be or later became a Labor politician, but because a long time ago she acted as a solicitor for an official who was successively Western Australian State Secretary and Victorian State Secretary of the AWU ... I viewed her as a very good witness in almost all respects. Many, many findings favourable to her and rejecting the attacks of her numerous critics were made ...
>
> Similarly, Mr Shorten was not called to give evidence because of anything he did as a Labor politician ... the point is that assessment of what trade union officials did at a particular time is not affected either by their political role at those times or by their later adoption of a political career ...

Not canvassed by the old lawyer was the possibility that Gillard and Shorten may have been before him for the political purposes of the Liberal Party. There was no contest here between the government and the unions, he declared. His terms of reference expressed no animus towards trade unions. "They seek not to destroy unions or obstruct their purposes, but to see whether they have been fulfilled and to see how they might be better fulfilled in future."

And it was a wonder to watch the mighty machinery of his mind reach the conclusion that the dinner was not even a Liberal Party event. Though organised by two branches of the Liberal Party made up of lawyers; though described to Heydon as the flagship event of those branches; though the invitation came with advertising for the party and invitations to make political donations to the party; it could not be called a Liberal Party event "in any substantively useful sense," because it was also open to the public. Non-Liberals could come and listen to his "points of possible curiosity" about the former Chief Justice. Not being exclusively Liberal, the event was not Liberal at all.

Heydon recusing himself would have been a mighty victory for Shorten. This result was more muddled. Commentators who for days had been saying Heydon had to go immediately declared that him staying was inevitable. News Corp swung heavily behind the commission. The government attacked Heydon's union critics as having crimes to hide. But Heydon's work is tainted now, not just by accepting a silly invitation to talk to Liberals about Barwick, but by the naive protestations in his 25,000 reasons, which will be pilloried all the way to election day 2016. Battle was being engaged as this essay went to press. The first forum will be the Senate, and the second, perhaps, the courts. Shorten said: "Everything the royal commission says may as well have a Liberal Party logo stamped on it."

He is the master of a small room. This is a boardroom in a Sydney ware-house, where an outfit called BlueChilli aims to turn start-ups into businesses. It's as elegant as all get-out. Everyone is young. They're in a rush to go places even when they're standing still. Shorten is shown around: bare brick, coffee machines and whiteboards. He says: "Where's the ping-pong table?" The language around the table is twenty-first-century but the ask is as old as time: these tyro entrepreneurs want government help. Shorten is a convincing listener. His questions are sharp: "How does it make money?" When the jargon becomes opaque he calls for a translation. "Unicorns?" The one-in-a-million success. "Moon shoot?" The vision that electrifies a community. This idea seems to give him pause. He commits not a cent in that half-hour but farewells a happy room. "I promise we'll have a good policy, because you'll help to write it."

Shorten has been two years in the job. The mathematics were daunting when he began. In 2013 Labor suffered its worst defeat since the Depression. Rudd saved the party maybe fifteen seats but Shorten needs another twenty-two to govern. He insists he has no regret for the bloodletting that brought the party to this point: "We do retain the capacity to be an effective Opposition." There were good reasons for him not to seek the leadership. He was young. He had time. The Australian people barely knew him. And he knows how bleak the outlook is for leaders who take over once their party has been thrown out of office. A Labor veteran says:

> It's very hard to lead in Opposition. It's especially hard to lead in the first term after you've been in government. Your record of government is going to be flung back at you every day. The task of persuading the electorate that they were wrong three years ago is always very great if you look at history.
>
> You're really accepting a two-term strategy with deep confidence in your abilities to manage a disparate rumbling caucus and

a bristling, insincerely loyal frontbench for six years. Faux matey-ness over the chopsticks. Gripes and grievances behind closed doors.

But the man who had for so long said he wanted to be leader could not back away. As much as anything, it was a question of credibility. If he flinched, how could he ever be believed again? On the Thursday after Rudd's defeat, Shorten called a press conference to confirm rumours he would be standing. The field was clearer than it might have been: Combet was ill and had left parliament. Chris Bowen, only forty, was willing to bide his time. But next day the Left's Anthony Albanese entered the contest. He was the favourite. A senior figure on the Right told Phil Coorey of the *Financial Review*: "Bill will get slaughtered."

What followed was the most civilised contest in Labor's history. Kevin Rudd's parting gift to the party was a radical protocol for making and breaking its leaders. After decades of empty talk about opening Labor to its members, something had finally been done. Under Rudd's new rules, hefty majorities of caucus would be needed to sack the leader: 75 per cent for a prime minister and 60 per cent for a leader of the Opposition. The plan was to outlaw ambush by faction. And when the time came for Labor to find a new leader, the rank and file would have an equal say with caucus. "The mechanisms," said Rudd, "prevent anyone from just wandering in one day, or one night, and saying, 'OK, sunshine, it's over.'"

For a month, the candidates were scrupulously polite to one another. They made almost identical policy pledges. Shorten suddenly discovered he had to extend his range, working out where he stood on issues that had barely troubled him in the past. Apart from differences over party reform — Albanese was calling on Labor to go further to break the power of the factions — the two were in such accord that the Left accused Shorten of deliberately "out Albo-ing Albo." To the commentators' surprise, Shorten won the set-piece debates comfortably. His opponent had stinging one-liners but Shorten found passion: "If I was to be PM, I would like to be known as the PM for the powerless, for the disempowered, for people who don't have a voice in society." Both men turned up at a barbecue breakfast in Perth to be questioned by officials of the CFMEU. Shorten pledged not to give back to the building industry watchdog, the Australian Building and Construction Commission, its old inquisitorial powers. "We like what you've said so far," remarked union official Joe McDonald. "Don't fuck it up."

Albanese won 18,230 rank-and-file votes. Shorten collected only 12,196 but had the numbers in caucus. "They broke arms and legs to lock in the vote for Shorten," said one veteran MP. The factions were still in disarray after Gillard's sacking, but the Right came together to back Shorten. A handful of Left MPs also drifted across to give him a big majority. His 64 per cent of the caucus outweighed Albanese's 60 per cent of the rank and file. Commentators made much of him not being the people's choice, but that caucus majority made him secure. There was no huge enthusiasm for him in the party. He was not seen as a miracle worker. But he was bricked in to the job. Yet his response to victory was drab. He barely celebrated. He seemed to shrink. Something had happened.

On the day he nominated for the leadership in September, a woman known as Kathy posted a message on Kevin Rudd's Facebook page, beneath his farewell message to the nation. She said Shorten "did things to me without my permission" at a camp in Portarlington twenty-seven years earlier. "You probably get crazy messages all the time," she wrote, "but I need help. Thankyou again for everything and I am sorry that the ALP did this to you too." The cartoonist Larry Pickering published her story on the net. Her allegations were detailed: she was sixteen, Shorten was nineteen, and a great deal of booze and some dope were involved the night she said he raped her in the bathroom of one of the cabins. She told Pickering she complained twice to the police: once in New South Wales in 2004, and again in Queensland in 2006 after she saw Shorten on television at Beaconsfield. She abandoned both complaints. Pickering believed her but was frank about her confusion and distress: "I assisted Kathy to her car and returned to my cramped office wondering how different Kathy's life might have been if Bill Shorten had never been born.

To be honest, I am not certain it would have been."

The rape allegation was there all through the leadership contest and would remain unresolved for the first year of Shorten's leadership. In the bifurcated world of the modern media, he was named everywhere on the net but nowhere in the press. The Coalition showed remarkable tact. Shorten engaged one of Australia's smartest lawyers, Leon Zwier of Arnold Bloch Leibler, who issued blunt denials in November 2013 after the *Australian* published the first, careful story about "a senior Labor figure" accused of rape:

> Lawyers for the man said last night the "unsubstantiated claims date back almost 30 years and they have never previously been raised with him". "The unsubstantiated claims are absolutely without foundation and are distressing for his family and for him," the lawyers said. "He strongly denies any wrongdoing and will fully cooperate with any investigation. Police have not contacted him."

Shorten is tough. His eagerness and charm mask this but those who have worked with him over the years agree he is exceptionally resilient. But the rape allegation crushed him just as he was coming to grips with his new role. He had not, until this time, been a big figure in Labor's national affairs. He had a great deal to call on – his native skill as a recruiter, his talent for healing wounded institutions, his genius with numbers – but he also had a great deal to learn. Any leader comes to office with debts. Yet a lifetime of faction plays meant he had to feel his way forward with particular care. Shorten owed so much to so many. He aged. Something of his old panache disappeared. And in the New Year, a few weeks after the police finally interviewed him about Kathy's allegation, his mother suddenly died.

"I feel loss, and I feel I do not know when I will not feel loss," he said at her funeral a week later. His dedication to his mother was profound. All his life he has explained himself by talking about Ann McGrath – never his father, who kept the ships moving in and out of Duke and Orr, but the resolute girl from Ballarat who made her own future. His father had disappeared from their lives even before he abandoned his marriage when the boys were in their late teens. The son admits despising him. Shorten is one of that interesting pack of politicians born of determined mothers and largely absent fathers. There are so many: Barack Obama, Bill Clinton and Tony Blair are distinguished alumni. Among recent Labor leaders in Australia are Rudd, Albanese and Shorten. Among the qualities these men share are self-discipline, boundless ambition and an appetite for approval on a national scale.

The funeral at Xavier was a great gathering of family, academics and Labor leaders, with two priests in charge: Frank Brennan for the Catholics and the Shortens' Anglican from Moonee Ponds. "He did the homily," says Brennan, "and I did the mass." Shorten was stricken. Brennan saw "a very emotional, filial individual paying tribute to the public and private undertakings of a mother devoted to the cause of education as a source of justice for all."

She had raised her twins to be liked and to win. When he has to choose, Bill opts for winning but the tension between the two is old and deep. It leaves him hungry for reassurance. So many stories are told about Shorten the union official, the cabinet minister and the leader of the party asking: "How did I go?" He still wears the face his mother gave him, the face of a boy who wants to be liked. It's a charming mask that hides too much for his own good. This man would be more respected if, like Hawke, Keating and Howard, he let us see the bastard that's in there. Instead, the rough edges are politely hidden. Perhaps this is the instinct of a kid from not quite the right side of the tracks who lands in a place like Xavier. "Don't let your heads be turned," Ann told her boys. She meant that. "She believed in merit," Shorten said at the funeral. "She taught me that merit is a legitimate human condition. That people should not be deified because of some ill-defined birth right or the wealth of an individual." But she also taught her sons to be polite and careful, to be good boys. There is about Shorten still a faint sense that he is a suitor in the world he wants to lead.

For a time he retreated to mourn. Months later, a photograph of his mother was on the fridge when Annabel Crabb brought the *Kitchen Cabinet* crew to Moonee Ponds for the awkward business of watching him cook ratatouille. Taking about Ann led him naturally to another big issue in his life: rivalry. "I thought my brother must have been better at the piano for no other reason than I thought it," he said, stirring the eggplant for the cameras. "When you're a twin, of course you *never* compete." He was delighted to bump into his old piano teacher Joyce Haslem at the funeral. "I said to Joyce, who was better at the piano? And Joyce said, *not* my brother. I haven't told him that. I realise it's naughty of me. It's naughty." He laughs like a little boy. Shorten is deeply competitive. Beating a staffer at five hundred fills him with glee. On *Kitchen Cabinet* he gave the impression that his mother was, along with everything else, the presiding genius of competition in his life. A few years before her death, talking to News Corp's Andrew Rule, she delivered a gnomic assessment of her two boys:

> At the end of a couple of hours, the conversation turned back to her sons. Rob, the quiet and steady banker, was more like her side of the family, she thought. And Bill, the mercurial one? She thought about it a while, rubbing her old dog's ears then said, "Bill … Bill is more like his father."

She did not live to see the news in August that her son would not be charged with rape. After ten months' investigation and on advice from the Office of Public Prosecutions, Victoria Police decided not to lay charges: "There was no reasonable prospect of conviction." The *Australian* broke the story on 21 August under the headline "Labor figure cleared in rape case." Kathy told reporter Dan Box, "How am I feeling? Angry, really, really angry." That afternoon, Shorten held a press conference to identify himself as the accused Labor figure:

> I fully co-operated to clear my name. And that is what I have done … the police have now concluded the investigation. The decision speaks for itself. It is over … I think in all fairness I have the

right to draw the line on this. I have no intention of making any further comment.

Shorten's colleagues rallied around him. In October Kathy engaged Melbourne QC Peter Faris and there was talk of her bringing a civil suit. That has not materialised and Shorten believes there is no prospect that it will. A year has passed. The closer the elections, the greater the risk the courts would regard any suit as an abuse of process. Coalition attack ads have not, at the time this essay went to press, alluded in any way to Kathy's allegation. It doesn't emerge even in hostile focus groups. The case is closed.

*

After he's put on a white coat to inspect super-efficient solar panels at the University of New South Wales, we have coffee in a city cafe. He has a sweet tooth and a little gut to match. He jogs, and he shows me an app that records his laps round Canberra's parliamentary triangle. He's fitter now than he seems in old footage of his union days and reckons he's beaten Abbott once or twice on fun runs. The idea pleases him. But he wants a serious word: "If your yarn is about Bill Shorten the factional operator, I don't think that really captures what's going on. It's part of my history I've worked through. But you know, the games are not worth doing if they're just for the sake of the games."

He's in a big-picture mood. There's a book on the way. Memoirs? "No, what I stand for." Before the election? "In an ideal world." He riffs about his politics, he doesn't use the language of the shop floor or the hustings. It's faintly New Age: "I fundamentally believe that if you empower people, you can move mountains. I fundamentally believe that if people are given a fair go, the world's a better place, people are happier individually and society progresses." He says he's grown. "I've learnt along the way. I'm a different person at forty-eight than I was at twenty-eight and certainly different to who I was at eighteen." So what does he know now that he didn't know then? "First, you've got to back yourself in. You don't wait for everyone else to agree, because that's not the way of progress. Second, I always ask myself: what will this look like in ten years' time? You worry about tomorrow, but you've got to ask: what will this look like in ten or twenty years' time?"

Not for the first time in these weeks, Shorten talks Napoleon. It is surprising how often he cites military rather than political thinkers. He tells me he admires John Monash for carrying out such meticulous preparation before every attack on the Western Front. But Napoleon is his hero and over coffee he once again cites the Corsican's maxim: find your enemy's weakest point and concentrate your attack there. That would be Tony Abbott. Yet the great question hanging over Shorten is whether he can, in fact, take the fight up to Abbott. In the rolling catastrophe of the Coalition government, most of the damage done to the prime minister has been self-inflicted. Another of Napoleon's maxims comes to mind: never interfere with an enemy in the process of destroying himself.

Shorten is by instinct a deal-maker. This explains a good deal of the difficulty he faces cutting through as leader of the Opposition. At the AWU he stacked on disputes and they could be willing. But the point was always to settle. And he was known then – and later as a minister – for reaching settlements that left all sides reasonably happy. His critics say he settles soft. If the top job is ever his, being a fine networker, recruiter and deal-maker will stand Shorten in great stead. But getting there is a different matter. A leader of the Opposition's task is to cultivate division. Abbott proved a genius at that. But Shorten struggles often to subdue the agreement demon in his nature. He has defined differences between the sides. He has defended Medicare, pensioners, the unemployed and university students. He is a republican who backs equal marriage. Labor under Shorten has pledged to continue the fight against climate change:

> We were right to support an emissions trading scheme. We were right to establish the Climate Change Authority, the Clean Energy Finance Corporation and the Australian Renewable Energy Target.

For this, we do not apologise. From this, we do not resile. We are not sceptics. We believe in the science.

But where Abbott is most himself, Shorten has beaten a retreat. "For Labor, national security is – and always will be – above politics," he says but what he means is that Labor will buckle whenever the government declares security is at stake. No political capital will be spent protecting liberty and the rule of law. Labor has tinkered with Abbott's security legislation but in the end has supported every measure: for the retention of metadata; prison for reporting ASIO "special" operations; broadening the already wide offence of "advocating" terrorism; retaining control and preventative detention orders; and stripping dual nationals of their Australian citizenship without trial or conviction.

What will it look like in ten years' time, I ask, that Labor passed a law to throw doctors and nurses in prison for reporting what they see on Manus and Nauru? "We will stand by them," he replies indignantly. But Labor voted for the Border Force Act and that's exactly what it does. "I don't share that interpretation." This is utterly baffling. Once dragged into court, nurses and social workers may have some whistle-blower protection but Labor voted to drag them there. Labor has voted for secrecy. Shorten has no idea how the camps will be cleared. He acknowledges that endorsing push-backs at the National Conference in July was only the latest in a long line of catch-ups with the Coalition's refugee policies. But he is confident Labor won't be forced to go any further: the worst has been reached. But isn't that what Labor always says? "Time will tell but I know that if we want more humanity in our system, I'll do a better job than the other fellow."

I am writing the last pages of this essay a few days after a wave of mockery compelled the Australian Border Force to abandon Operation Fortitude – a plan to send its gorgeously uniformed officers out to check the visa status of "any individual we cross paths with" in the streets of Melbourne. Did Shorten speak for the nation when he heard about this scheme? No, he spoke for a party terrified of the wedge. "If you're going to do a blitz," he said solemnly, "I don't know why you'd necessarily telegraph it to the media first." Demonstrators rallied at Flinders Street station, and within a couple of hours Operation Fortitude was canned. Only then did Shorten find his voice to condemn "one of the most catastrophically silly ideas I've seen this government do ... I don't think there's a single Victorian and indeed a single Australian whose jaw just didn't hit the ground ... truly, how dumb is this government some days?" Once he was safe, he was magnificent.

Bob Hawke is the only prime minister since Chifley to come from the trade union movement. The Coalition line is that Hawke was a hero but the last of his kind. Bill Kelty scoffs at this: "It was really hard for Hawke. People glorify the bastard and forget what they said about him." He does not believe the ground rules have shifted against unionists. But Hawke left the unions behind. "Bill is different," says Kelty. "He hasn't resigned the factions."

Shorten is still a player, and the factions are a mess. The Stability Pact that was supposed to last a generation broke down at Rudd's restoration. Shorten was punished. All of his picks for parliamentary real estate in the 2013 election were foiled. Gillard's seat he wanted to go to Andrew Landeryou's wife, Kimberley Kitching. Gillard blocked that. He then tried to put Kitching into the Senate. Conroy blocked that. His candidate for Simon Crean's old seat lost out when Conroy and the NUW both sided against him. Since that time, Shorten and Conroy have made up. These days it's more a marriage of convenience, but the ShortCons matter again. And the numbers games go on, more ferocious than ever as party membership and union membership dwindle. Talent is finding it harder than before to defeat the machine. Shorten knows that, as Labor leader, he has to present some agenda for party reform. No one can defend the system as it is. But he is only talking modest cuts to union numbers on panels that select Labor candidates. There are no firm proposals and no timetable for change. Shorten is not going to throw the party open to the rank and file.

If Australia has to endure a union man as prime minister, it's hard to imagine a more congenial candidate than Shorten. He represents nil challenge to capitalism. He is AWU not CFMEU. Since he birched Latham a decade ago for veering too far left, Shorten has stuck to the middle ground. His politics are blue-collar conservative. If he is proposing policies now that were fringe back then – like marriage equality and renewable energy – it's not because he has shifted. They have moved to the centre, where he has always been standing. He has no radical designs, no great plans for reform. His goal is power for Labor and Bill Shorten, and decent administration for Australia.

Shorten's colleagues reckon he is doing well. The stumbling of the first months has gone. He's finding his feet. No one pretends he is setting Australia on fire, but he's not making mistakes. He's cautious. Labor hopes we are getting the message that he is a safe pair of hands. The party is at peace. There are no whispers against his leadership. He is even more secure now than he was when he defeated Albanese. "I know there is more goodwill towards me at the moment in the party than there has been," he says. "It develops over time." But Australia has not come to share his party's regard for Shorten. When pollsters ask us who we would like to lead the government and the Opposition, we answer Malcolm Turnbull and Someone Else. That's a grim verdict, but Shorten has Abbott on his side. From the moment of Abbott's victory, there crept over the country what the pollster Andrew Catsaras calls "a sombre mood of buyer's remorse." Regret and disillusionment became the primary emotions of the nation's politics. The last time the two-party-preferred vote favoured the Coalition was in October 2013. The message of the polls is that an election held on just about any Saturday in the last two years would have seen Australia go back to Labor. Abbott's government cannot be written off, but at this point it seems a unique failure.

We are, in so many ways, where we were three years ago. An Opposition leader who is not much admired faces a government that has lost its way. The Opposition is disciplined. The government is in disarray. The recurring political question is: can the prime minister survive? Abbott was a superb Opposition leader, far more dynamic than Shorten could ever be. Yet he was as hard for the electorate to read in 2013 as Shorten is now.

With Abbott the question was whether he could outgrow the narrow values that powered his career. The answer turned out to be no. With Shorten the question is not so very different: can he rise above the machine politics that brought him to the top? There is no doubt he would have made a fine premier of Victoria. But does Bill Shorten scale up? "I look forward to demonstrating that. I know what the nation should look like in ten and fifteen years' time and it's up to me to tell that story to the nation. My job isn't to convince Tony Abbott or News Limited that they should vote for me. My job is to convince Australians I have a plan for the future."

SOURCES

Bill Shorten gave me time and documents, for which I am most grateful. Colleagues from his many lives — schoolboy to leader of the Opposition — helped me on and off the record to grasp the shape of his complicated life.

But this essay would not have been possible without the labour over many years of my colleagues, particularly in the Melbourne press, who tracked the wild factional plays that are at the heart of Shorten's career. Of that big team, I want to thank particularly Jason Koutsoukis, Ewin Hannan, Brad Norington and the splendid Michael Bachelard. At the end of my desk is a wall of books about the Rudd–Gillard era. Over the last months I have regularly given thanks for the memoirs of Gillard, Combet and Rob Oakeshott; the diaries of Bob Carr; Paul Kelly's *Triumph and Demise*, Aaron Patrick's *Downfall* and Barrie Cassidy's *The Party Thieves*.

Russell Marks, lawyer and policy advisor, recruited his La Trobe colleague Dominic Kelly, doctoral candidate and political commentator, to a two-man research team of great skill and endless energy. They were my seeing-eye dogs in the dark world of Victorian politics.

And this is something I've never done before: thank Chris Feik, my infinitely demanding editor at Black Inc., for dragging another Quarterly Essay out of me.

Transcripts for the Royal Commission into Trade Union Governance and Corruption can be accessed at www.tradeunionroyalcommission.gov.au/Hearings/Documents/Transcripts/2015/Transcript-8-July-2015.pdf (8 July) and www.tradeunionroyalcommission.gov.au/Hearings/Documents/Transcripts/2015/Transcript-9-July-2015.pdf (9 July).

3   "I don't hate": Shorten to me, 30 July 2015.
6   "That smirking phoney": *Hansard*, 19 August 2015, pp. 47–8.
7   "I have suggested": William Shorten, Royal Commission on the Activities of the Federated Ship Painters and Dockers Union, 3 February 1981, p. 754.
7–8 "Look it up", "Because it's quicker", "There was politics" and "The breadth of": Shorten's eulogy for his mother, 15 April 2014, text supplied by Shorten.
9   "This, from the beginning": Letter from Fr Pedro Arrupe SJ, 20 May 1978, *Xaverian* (Xavier College), December 1978, p. 5.
9   "Don't let your heads be turned": Shorten's eulogy, 15 April 2014.
9   "outstanding contribution" and "William proved": *Xaverian*, 1983, pp. 30 & 39.
9   "He was always": Chris Gleeson to me, 23 June 2015.

10   "We were all very": John Roskam to me, 24 June 2015.

10   "The house meetings": *Xaverian*, 1984, p. 28.

10   "I've always been" and all other quotations from Des King: To me, 6 July 2015.

11   "He is breaking": Race Mathews to me, 25 June 2015.

11   "I was a": "Insight", *Age*, 24 September 2009, p. 1.

11   "I chose to": Shorten to me, 16 July 2015.

11   "I wasn't really": Shorten to me, 30 July 2015.

11   "Our spies also": *Lot's Wife*, 7 September 1985, p. 15.

12   "In reply to": *Lot's Wife*, vol. 25, no. 8, p. 15.

12   "The Socialist Left": *Sunday Age*, 28 May 2006, p. 13.

12   "Network had one": Aaron Patrick, *Downfall: How the Labor Party Ripped Itself Apart*, ABC Books, 2013, p. 13.

12   "Bill was just": Patrick to me, 21 July 2015.

12–13 "Get all your mates" and "It was about": Peter Cowling to me, 24 June 2015.

13   "If he wasn't": Roskam to me, 24 June 2015.

13   "A sport where": *Sunday Age*, 28 May 2006, p. 13.

14   "In your last": *Lot's Wife*, 28 July 1986, p. 27.

14   "a festival of" and "spiteful screaming matches": *Lot's Wife*, 23 June 1986, p. 7.

15   "I know they say" and other Shorten quotes on this page: To me, 30 July 2015.

15   "legitimate market research": *Lot's Wife*, 15 June 1987, p. 3.

16   "They spent a couple": Patrick, *Downfall*, p. 19.

16   "As a former Young": Christina Cridland, *Sunday Times*, Perth, 16 June 2013, p. 67.

16–17 "You can't keep" and "Politics is a": Shorten to me, 30 July 2015.

17   "We were cheesed": Information to me.

17   "I enjoyed his": Julia Gillard, *My Story*, Knopf, 2014, p. 417.

17–18 "He was active" and "John Cain Junior": Testimony of Robert Kernohan to the Royal Commission into Trade Union Governance and Corruption, 11 June 2014, www.tradeunionroyalcommission.gov.au/Hearings/Documents/Transcripts/ turc-transcript-public-hearing-11june2014.pdf, pp. 369 & 370.

18–19 "From the time" and all other Peter Koutsoukis quotes: To me, 7 July 2015.

18   "A lawyer with": *Age*, 2 April 1994, p. 1.

18   "Mr Kernohan said": *Financial Review*, 9 July 1992, p. 4.

19   "Where someone has": Shorten to me, 8 July 2015.

19   "He was very young" and "I told him": Bill Kelty to me, 22 July 2015.

19   "When I was": *Hansard*, 14 February 2008, p. 328.

20   "to shine": Tony Abbott, joint press conference, 10 February 2014, www.pm.gov. au/media/2014-02-10/joint-press-conference-attorney-general-and-minister- employment-parliament-house.

21   "Instead of securing": Jeremy Stoljar, Counsel Assisting Opening Statement, Royal Commission, 28 May 2015, www.tradeunionroyalcommission.gov.au/Hearings/Documents/Transcripts/2015/Transcript-28-May-2015.pdf, p. 7.

21   "I thought it was": Ben Davis's testimony, Royal Commission, 4 June 2015, www.tradeunionroyalcommission.gov.au/Hearings/Documents/Transcripts/2015/Transcript-4-June-2015.pdf, p. 648.

22   "dudding their workers": *Alan Jones Breakfast Show*, Radio 2GB, 11 June 2015, www.pm.gov.au/media/2015-06-11/interview-alan-jones-radio-2gb-sydney.

23   "There is no way" and "I don't micromanage": Shorten's testimony, Royal Commission, 8 July 2015, pp. 58 & 16.

23   "I don't know" and "I would never": Shorten's testimony, 9 July 2015, pp. 59 & 113.

23–4 "You, if I can" and "You may or": Dyson Heydon, Royal Commission, 9 July 2015, pp. 136 & 201.

24   "This hurt him": Kelty to me, 22 July 2015.

25   "The old AWU": Shorten to me, 8 July 2015.

25   "A lot of people": *Age*, 3 April 1995, p. 8.

25–6 "We are all": *Age*, 19 June 1997, p. 18.

26   "It wasn't doable": Shorten to me, 30 July 2015.

26   "Shorten cut me": Kernohan's witness statement, paragraph 134.

27   "He has had": Royal Commission into Trade Union Governance and Corruption Interim Report, vol. 1, paragraph 294, www.tradeunionroyalcommission.gov.au/reports/Documents/InterimReportVol1.pdf.

27   "Do the people" and "Steve Bracks said": Shorten to me, 8 July 2015.

27   "I could have": Patrick, *Downfall*, p. 190.

27–8 "I listen to" etc: Shorten to me, 30 July 2015.

28   "You've got to be": Kelty to me, 22 July 2105.

29   "Trade union officials": BRW, 14 December 1998, p. 46.

29   "Esso makes $1 million": *Age*, 31 July 2001, p. 2.

29   "a mixture of": *Herald Sun*, 21 April 2001, p. 27.

29   "It's like bringing": *Herald Sun*, 24 March 2000, p. 20.

30   "The first thing": *Herald Sun*, 21 April 2001, p. 27.

30   "Shorten, who is": BRW, 22 June 2001, p. 18.

31   "You're asking for": Shorten's testimony, 9 July 2015, pp. 128–9.

31   "Whilst I was": Shorten's testimony 8 July 2015.

31   "What profoundly weakens": Shorten's testimony, 9 July 2015, p. 189.

31   "Generally speaking": Stoljar, 28 May 2015, p. 6.

32   "Are you able" etc: Stoljar and Shorten, 8 July 2015, p. 103.

32   "If you and I": Shorten's testimony, 8 July 2015, p. 82.

32 "highly unlikely that": Shorten's testimony, 8 July 2015, p. 65.

33 "Nothing untoward about" and "Unions have been": Shorten's testimony, 9 July 2015, pp. 126 & 121.

33 "This is a long way": *Sydney Morning Herald*, 27 October 2003, p. 6.

33 "If the company": Shorten's testimony, 9 July 2015, pp. 126 & 117.

33 "It was the idea": Shorten's testimony, 8 July 2015, p. 87.

33–4 "I had a lot": Shorten's testimony, 9 July 2015, p. 156

34 "Isn't this really": Stoljar, 9 July 2015, p. 163.

34 "They have to be": Shorten's testimony, 8 July 2015, p. 86.

35 "Tollway workers": *Age*, 10 March 2005, p. 9.

35 "It was a big": Shorten's testimony, 9 July 2015, p. 114.

35 "I cannot speak": Shorten's testimony, 9 July 2015, p. 123.

35 AWU ball etc: MFI – 9, Thiess John Holland, Royal Commission, evidence presented, 9 July 2015.

36 "a very good": Shorten, 9 July 2015, p. 113.

36–7 "Did you discuss" etc: Stoljar and Shorten, 9 July 2015, p. 118.

38 "I was a union": Shorten to me, 30 July 2015.

38–43 "A lot of" and all other Shaun Micallef quotes: To me, 29 July 2015.

39–43 "I'd Like to Teach the World to Zing": Script provided by Shaun Micallef.

41 "It is like": *Hansard*, 9 February 2015, p. 80.

41 "These people opposite" and "Treasurer Hockey": *Sydney Morning Herald*, 2 December 2014, http://www.smh.com.au/federal-politics/political-news/bill-shorten-mocks-bill-shorten-over-infamous-zingers-20141202-11yhhz.html.

41 "If I can borrow": *Australian*, 17 January 2015, p. 20.

42 "We have now": *Australian*, 22 January 2015, p. 9.

42 "Which is pleasing": *Sydney Morning Herald*, 2 December 2014.

44 "And the last": *Australian*, 20 September 2005, p. 2.

45 "How low can": Mark Latham, *The Latham Diaries*, MUP, 2005, p. 138.

45 "It was the beginning": Race Mathews to me, 25 June 2015.

46 "As right-wing": *Age*, 22 April 1985, p. 1.

46 "His opponents use": *Australian Financial Review*, 18 March 2006, p. 26.

47 "They were the": Shorten to me, 30 July 2015.

47 "If the NUW": *Age*, 8 July 2000, p. 9.

48 "We recognise unions": *Age*, 20 July 2001, p. 3.

48 "How about simply": *Age*, 21 July 2001, p. 6.

48 "His flag is": *Crikey*, 4 June 2002, www.crikey.com.au/2002/05/26/delia-delegate-dishes-dirt-doozies/?wpmp_switcher=mobile&wpmp_tp=4.

48–9 "When I first": Latham, *The Latham Diaries*, p. 297.

49   "I said that": Latham, *The Latham Diaries*, p. 318.

49   "The key challenge": *Australian*, 21 July 2004, p. 15.

49–50 "Yet the Howard" and "There is a problem": Shorten, address to the National Press Club, 27 February 2002, http://worksite.econ.usyd.edu.au/shorten.html.

50–1 "Labor's task now": *Arena*, 1 December 2004, www.thefreelibrary.com/The+new+centre.-a0126787732.

51   "absolute horseshit": Latham, *The Latham Diaries*, 24 Friday 2004, p. 14.

51   "a magnificent achievement": *Age*, 13 February 2004, p. 2.

51   "The resulting alliance": *Australian*, 26 November 2005, p. 23.

52   "I do think": *Australian*, 6 June 2005, p. 2.

52–3 "There are no": Greg Combet to me, 25 August 2015.

53   "It throws up": Gerry Kitchener to me, 24 June 2015.

53   "What is democratic": *Age*, 19 March 2005, p. 3.

54   "I'm not going": *Age*, 16 March 2005, p. 3.

54   "Richard Marles explained": *Australian*, 26 January 2006, p. 2.

55   "I've done everything": *Australian*, 15 March 2006, p. 2.

56   "one of our thinkers": *Australian*, 24 October 2005, p. 2.

56   "a branch-stacking oaf": *Crikey*, 26 May 2002.

57   "To continually promote" and "He is the next": *Sunday Age*, 21 June 2015, p. 7.

57   "We haven't won": Campaign letter, *Age*, 4 February 2006, p. 6.

57   "The OC notes": *The Other Cheek*, 27 August 2005, http://pandora.nla.gov.au/pan/64343/20061130-0000/andrewlanderyou.blogspot.com/2005_08_27_andrewlanderyou_archive.html.

58   "Sercs made an": Andrew Landeryou, 28 July 2005, http://pandora.nla.gov.au/pan/64343/20061130-0000/andrewlanderyou.blogspot.com/2005_07_28_andrewlanderyou_archive.html.

58   "He's hard-working": *Age*, 4 February 2006, p. 6.

58   "The old saying": *Australian*, 19 August 2005, p. 7.

58   "The central problem": *Australian Financial Review*, 7 February 2006, p. 53.

58   "He's not the": *Australian*, 22 February 2006, p. 1.

60   "He's a capable": *Mercury*, 13 May 2006, p. 3.

60   "He wants to be PM": Information to me.

60   "Bill Shorten likes": "Insight", *Age*, 12 November 2005, p. 3.

60   "It really drives": Information to me.

62   "Bill for PM": *Daily Telegraph*, 16 May 2006, p. 1.

62   "throwing a Kleenex": Shorten, quoted in the *Canberra Times*, 10 May 2006, p. 2.

62   "that you continue": Tony Wright, *Bad Ground: Inside the Beaconsfield Mine Rescue—The Brant Webb & Todd Russell Story*, 2009, p. 287.

62   "We cannot afford": *Sydney Morning Herald*, 11 May 2006, p. 15.

62   "He gave, too": Bob Ellis, *And So It Went*, Penguin, 2009, p. 214.

63   Leadership support: ACNielsen Poll, 21 May 2006.

63   "to ring me": Bob Sercombe, quoted in the *Australian*, 17 May 2006, p. 2.

63   "Maribyrnong was what": Shorten's testimony, 8 July 2015 , p. 6.

63   "The AWU was": Shorten's testimony, 8 July 2015, p. 26.

63–4 "re-emerged as an": *Australian*, 1 March 2006, p. 6.

64   "Unions can waste": *Australian Financial Review*, 25 September 2007, p. 1.

64   "Mr Shorten said": *Australian Financial Review*, 16 November 2006, p. 3.

64   "Ted, would you": Shorten's testimony, 8 July 2015, p. 22.

64   "a bit of": Shorten's testimony, 8 July 2015, p. 30.

64   "a good cut": Shorten's testimony, 8 July 2015, p. 11.

65   "The idea that": Shorten's testimony, 8 July 2015, p. 25.

65   "He was a": Shorten's testimony, 8 July 2015, p. 6.

65   "When you're the": Shorten's testimony, 8 July 2015, p. 33.

65   "You will have": Shorten's testimony, 8 July 2015, p. 73.

65   "At the National": Shorten's testimony, 8 July 2015, p. 74.

66   "I can just": Shorten's testimony, 8 July 2015, p. 72.

66–7 "On the boards": *Hansard*, 14 February 2008, p. 328.

67   "I will be leading": *Australian*, 5 December 2006, p. 1.

67   "We've fixed Bill": Information to me.

67   "If you want" and 'This is going": Kelty to me, 22 July 2015.

67–8 "He just didn't": Information to me.

68   "People give you": *Sunday Age*, 23 November 2008, p. 21.

68   "It's nothing to": *Sunday Times* (Perth), 16 June 2013, p. 67.

68   "In the evening": *Courier-Mail*, 5 September 2007, p. 78.

69   "I believe in God", etc: Shorten to me, 30 July 2015.

69   "It was at the heart" and "When I hear": Shorten, speech to the Australian Christian Lobby, 25 October 2014, www.alp.org.au/shorten_acl_address.

70   "It is a bit": *Australian*, 20 January 2009, p. 5.

70   "Parliament was sitting": Kitchener to me, 24 June 2015.

70   "He actually fell": Gillard, *My Story*, p. 418.

71   "I wished the": *Age*, 4 May 2013, p. 5.

71   "That is what": *Australian Financial Review*, 15 February 2010, p. 60.

71-2 "Shorten makes no": Wikileaks, 12 June 2009, wikileaks.org/plusd/cables/09MELBOURNE69_a.html.

72   "That's what it's": Information to me.

73   "the last practical": *Sydney Morning Herald*, 24 November 2009, p. 4.

73   "in electoral trouble": Paul Kelly, *Triumph and Demise*, MUP, 2014, p. 10.

73   "We had to do": Shorten, on *Q&A*, ABC TV, 28 June 2010.

73   "He was dismayed": Barrie Cassidy, *The Party Thieves*, MUP, pp. 81–2.

73   "should think about this": Shorten, on ABC TV, *Q&A*, 28 June 2010.

74   "We're bloody stuffed": Sam Dastyari, *The Killing Season*, ABC TV, 16 June 2015.

74   "It was spontaneous": Kelly, *Triumph and Demise*, p. 10.

74   "I honestly don't": Kitchener to me, 24 June 2015.

74   "Don't mistake this": Information to me.

74   "infamous footage": Shorten to me, 30 July 2015.

75   "I am now advised": Kelly, *Triumph and Demise*, p. 326.

75   "Shorten was in": Kitchener, *The Killing Season*, ABC TV, episode 2, 16 June 2015.

75   "He was still": Kitchener to me, 24 June 2015.

75   "He said you couldn't": Kitchener, *The Killing Season*, ABC TV, episode 2, 16 June 2015.

77   "She wasn't one": Kitchener to me, 24 June 2015.

78   "The five peak": Rob Oakeshott, *The Independent Member for Lyne*, Allen & Unwin, 2014, p. 290.

78   "This week the": *Australian*, 17 December 2010, p. 12.

78   "Shorten brings to": Paul Barry, Power Index, www.thepowerindex.com.au/politicians/bill-shorten power index, 24 April 2012.

79   "I don't believe": *Australian*, 13 December 2011, p. 6.

79   "The union fox": *Australian Financial Review*, 13 December 2011, p. 1.

79   "This fucking language": www.youtube.com/watch?v=RkKTI_PHpjI.

80   "I support the": *Q&A*, ABC TV, 20 February 2012.

80   "Life's a journey": *Sunday Herald Sun*, 13 May 2012, p. 4.

80   "These matters are": *Age*, 27 April 2012, p. 1.

81   "Do you think": *Australian*, 27 April 2012, p. 13.

81   "Is Bill Shorten": *Guardian*, 27 April 2012, www.theguardian.com/world/short-cuts/2012/apr/27/bill-shorten-loyal-politician-australian.

81   "Shorten was clearly": *Sun Herald*, 29 April 2012, p. 81.

82   "a cheap political": *Age*, 27 April 2012, p. 2.

82   "I can't vote" etc: *Australian Financial Review*, 21 June 212, p. 1.

82–3 "I know the": *Australian Financial Review*, 22 June 2012, p. 1.

83   "That account was": *Lateline*, ABC TV, 21 November 2012.

84   "It's been a big": *Age*, 22 March 2013, p. 2.

84–5 "When governments are": Information to me.

85   "I support her": *Daily Telegraph*, 13 June 2013, p. 1.

85–6 "I hoped that" and "Because that's not": Shorten to me, 30 July 2015.

86   "Shorten wanted to" Kelly, *Triumph and Demise*, p. 468.

86   "I have now": *Australian Financial Review*, 27 June 2013, p. 8.

87–9 "for sensible reasons" and all other quotes: Dyson Heydon, Reasons for Ruling on Disqualification Applications, 31 August 2015, www.tradeunionroyalcommission.gov.au/Hearings/Documents/2015/Evidence31August2015/ReasonsforRulingonDisqualificationApplicationdated31August2015.pdf.

89   "Everything the royal": *Australian*, 1 September 2015, p. 1.

90   "We do retain": *Australian Financial Review*, 9 September 2013, p. 13.

90–1 "It's very hard": Information to me.

91   "Bill will get": *Australian Financial Review*, 12 September 2013, p. 1.

91   "The mechanisms": *Herald Sun*, 9 July 2013, p. 6.

91   "out Albo-ing": *Australian*, 28 September 2013, p. 8.

91–2 "If I was to": *Sydney Morning Herald*, 25 September 2013, p. 8.

92   "We like what": *Australian*, 1 October 2013, p. 4.

92   "They broke arms": Information to me.

92   "did things to" and "You probably get": This post was captured in a screengrab at https://kangaroocourtofaustralia.files.wordpress.com/2013/11/bill-shorten-rape-2-edited.jpg.

92–3 "I assisted Kathy": Larry Pickering, "I was raped by Bill Shorten," 16 September 2014, http://pickeringpost.com/story/-i-was-raped-by-bill-shorten-cont-/3803.

93   "Lawyers for the": *Australian*, 14 November 2013, p. 1.

93–4 "I feel loss" and "She believed in": Notes from Shorten's eulogy for his mother, delivered 15 April 2014, supplied by Shorten.

94   "He did the" and "a very emotional": Brennan to me, 22 August 2015.

95   "I thought my": *Kitchen Cabinet*, ABC TV, 4 November 2014.

95   "At the end": *Sunday Herald Sun*, 9 August 2015, p. 27.

95   "There was no" and "How am I": *Australian*, 21 August 2014, p. 3.

95–6 "I fully co-operated": Fragmented reports of his statement and answers – *Age*, 22 August 2014, p. 4; *Australian*, 22 August 2014, p. 2; *Herald Sun*, 4 October 2014, p. 2.

96   "If your yarn" and all subsequent Shorten quotes (unless otherwise indicated): To me, 30 July 2015.

97–8 "We were right": *Hansard*, 14 July 2014, p. 7697.

98   "For Labor": *Hansard*, 1 September 2014, p. 9148.

98–9 "If you're going": *Australian Financial Review*, 29 August 2015, p. 4.

99   "one of the": *New Matilda*, 30 August 2015.

99   "It was really" and "Bill is different": Kelty to me, 22 July 2015.

100   "a sombre mood": Andrew Catsaras, 21 August 2015, http://andrewcatsaras.blogspot.com.au

Hugh White

Quarterly Essay 58 tells an interesting story about the War on Terror, exploring how it has been conducted, how it has evolved and why it has failed so far, all illuminated by David Kilcullen's colourful accounts of his own role in it. But it also presents a policy argument about what should be done next. Like Tony Abbott, though apparently for different reasons, David sees ISIS as a deadly threat that must be eliminated, and like Abbott he argues that the West, including Australia, should commit armed forces to do this. The difference is that David thinks we need to be doing much more in Iraq than Abbott has so far signed up to. David argues for this by explaining why he thinks ISIS poses a threat to us, and why he thinks a bigger Western military intervention would remove that threat. Alas, I'm not sure either element of this argument is compelling.

Let's start by asking how ISIS threatens the West, and Australia specifically. David offers four answers (in the passage starting on page 69). First he mentions remote radicalisation – the danger that ISIS's example will inspire acts of terrorism at home. But as he says, this is not really a strategic threat to our societies, because the numbers killed are quite low. Of course it is a problem that needs to be taken seriously, but I think David agrees that it is best dealt with by good intelligence, policing and outreach here at home rather than by trying to fight ISIS in Iraq and Syria.

Second, he mentions the foreign fighter issue – the relatively large numbers of Westerners who have joined ISIS. It is not completely clear to me how David sees this as a threat to Australia or the West, though presumably his main concern, like Tony Abbott's, is that they will return with the skills and motivation to amplify the terrorist threat here at home. In this context David presents what he calls "the most persuasive reason for a forward strategy," which is that if we do not fight ISIS in the Middle East, then the measures to contain the consequent terrorist threat at home will turn our societies into police states. This argument is compelling only if we accept that the terrorist threat would otherwise be serious enough to warrant the kind of draconian measures he goes on to describe. But that has not been established. As so often since 2001, the potential for terrorism to pose an existential threat is assumed, when it needs to be demonstrated. Of course David might be suggesting that we are in danger of turning our nation into a police state even if the threat does not warrant it. That is indeed a risk, but the best way to avoid that risk is to have a more responsible, better-informed and less politically opportunistic debate at home, not to go off to fight more wars abroad.

Third, David mentions the potential for ISIS to inspire and support Islamist insurgencies elsewhere around the world. This too is a legitimate concern, but is it a big enough problem to warrant a large-scale military intervention in Iraq and Syria? That depends on how seriously these other insurgencies affect our interests, and how much difference ISIS support makes to them. The answers to these questions cannot be taken for granted.

Fourth, David argues that ISIS must be defeated to remove the threat of a general collapse of the Middle East regional order, including the real risk of full-scale war between the region's larger powers. This is indeed a major concern, and raises much more significant issues globally and for the West specifically than the other reasons David offers for another military intervention in the Middle East. But we need to be careful about assuming that ISIS is the cause of this problem and that destroying ISIS would remove it. ISIS itself is only a symptom and a consequence of bigger trends that are destroying the old post-Ottoman regional order in the Middle East, and there is no reason at all to believe that removing ISIS will restore that order, or prevent further instability and conflict.

The other question we have to consider is how likely it is that the military intervention David advocates would succeed in destroying ISIS. He is careful to argue that this would not be another counterinsurgency campaign like that in Afghanistan. That's because, he says, ISIS is not an insurgency but a state, and needs to be fought like a state. Nor does he argue that the West should deploy its own armies to defeat ISIS themselves. Instead it should do more – much more – of what it is already doing in Iraq: providing air support and training, advice and assistance to Iraqi forces so they can do the job themselves. In particular, he thinks Western military advisers need to accompany Iraqi forces into the fighting on the front-line.

But how likely is any of this to make a real difference in Iraq? For a long time now, people have assumed that Western training and example can turn ill-trained, under-motivated and unpaid soldiers into war winners. It very rarely works. Moreover, as David himself acknowledges, security assistance alone makes no difference without wider social, political and economic reforms, and what chance is there of those in Iraq today? No better than in Afghanistan five or ten years ago. So it is very unlikely that a larger Western intervention would do any good, and quite likely that it would do real harm, making the situation even worse. It would not be the first time that has happened, after all.

Better, then, to leave the Iraqis and their neighbours to sort this one out without our help. That does not mean sitting back while ISIS takes over the Middle East, of course, because ISIS is already contained by the powers it has come up against – Turkey, the Kurds, Iraqi Shi'as and of course Iran, as well as Sunni rivals and adversaries inside and outside Iraq and Syria. These are the forces that will determine the shape of the new Middle East and ISIS's role in it, and there is not much that we in the West can do to shape the outcome, so we should not try unless the imperative is much more compelling, and the means much more effective, than David's arguments suggest.

Of course this is an uncomfortable conclusion for those who believe in America's and the West's power to shape the world. That idea is being challenged today in the Middle East, as well as in Eastern Europe and East Asia. I suspect that this is the real reason why so many in the West find what is happening there so disconcerting. ISIS does not really threaten Australia or the West strategically in any substantial way, but it does threaten our assumption that the West can and should control what happens in the region.

That is why the most telling passage in David's Quarterly Essay is the one in which he warns that a US decision not to intervene against ISIS threatens the whole post-1945 global order. David worries that if America doesn't step in to defeat ISIS in the Middle East it will mark the end of this whole era in which America's ability and willingness to use its preponderant power has kept the world safe and stable. David's essay is infused with his confidence that the West, led by Washington, can still do this. But all the evidence, from Iraq, Afghanistan, Syria and Lebanon – as well as Iran, Ukraine, Georgia, North Korea and the South China Sea – shows that this era has already passed. Another sad and costly failure in Iraq would not bring it back.

Hugh White

Jim Molan

Barbara Tuchman, in her 1984 book *The March of Folly*, defined folly as governments pursuing policies contrary to their own interests, despite feasible alternatives. Much of the criticism of our ongoing involvement in Iraq is based on a view that what our governments are doing is Tuchman-style folly, especially when it is imagined that the alternative is to do nothing. We all know that governments can commit folly by pursuing the unworkable at the expense of the possible, one of the most common of governmental follies. If Tuchman were alive today, she might examine the First and Second Iraq Wars and the war in Afghanistan since 2001. But for fairness, she should also examine the folly of non-intervention in Syria and the less effective intervention in this, the Third Iraq War.

The best means of avoiding folly is to align strategy with tactics. David Kilcullen reminds us in his essay that strategy ensures that you get to the right place with the right force for the right reasons and in the right war. Victory is about achieving the war aims, but you must be able to both formulate a strategy and implement it.

So, whether or not government actions are considered folly, and whatever the question is, the answer is very likely to be strategy. Kilcullen covers the full, comprehensive scope of national strategy to combat the Islamic State. This is very important, because only a comprehensive strategy will ever produce results.

His essay reminded me that what passed for military strategy in both Iraq and Afghanistan was that we in the Coalition put in an inadequate number of troops initially, contrary to professional advice, found we were being beaten, increased the number of troops to what it should have been to begin with and called it a "Surge," and achieved the success that we should have achieved to begin with. Then, when things started to look much better, we prematurely reduced the number of troops and set a timetable for final withdrawal. As a result of inadequate strategy in Iraq, we had to create local forces, a process that was prolonged because we were not able to deploy, even initially, the right number of competent troops to create what must always come first: a degree of stability. Our inadequate strategy extended the war and the suffering, we are now back in Iraq, and the US president has accepted that he needs to leave a residual force of 10,000 US troops in Afghanistan so as not to lose everything that we have gained there, as is close to happening in Iraq.

The announcement of additional Australian troops to train Iraqis brought forth the usual suspects in public commentary. What very few addressed is the view that all of those who see ISIS as evil should be prepared, as part of an overall strategy, to commit military and other resources to oppose that evil. This conflict can be successfully concluded, but we need the Iraqis to carry the bulk of the fight. But to do so they need our assistance.

Our assistance to Iraq might be underdone, but should not at this stage include ground combat units, and definitely not of the previous magnitude. Yet "boots on the ground" should never be ruled out, because, as Kilcullen points out, it is in the interests of the West to win in Iraq and Syria. And we have as much of a moral obligation to assist the Iraqi government to regain sovereignty over areas currently held by ISIS as we had to provide humanitarian assistance on Mount Sinjar.

One of the salient differences between the Third Iraq War and the previous two is that the West is more directly in strategic competition with Iran. At the moment, as has been said, Iran is playing three-dimensional chess while the West is only just starting to play checkers. Iran's speed and effectiveness in supporting the Iraqis on the battlefield, and its willingness to mentor or advise in battle, may mean Iran will win the peace no matter who wins the war.

It is only eleven years since the invasion, perhaps too soon for a full formal analysis. But the Middle East does not wait, and what you learn will always depend on where you stand. For instance, had Secretary of Defense Rumsfeld listened to military advice on necessary troop levels before the invasion, we might have achieved in two years what it took eight years and two troop surges to achieve.

As Kilcullen points out, by 2011, when the coalition troops left, the US and Iraqi forces had brought about a relatively high level of stability, including a significant degradation of al-Qaeda in Iraq. The US forces that Kilcullen advised be deployed, and that some of us fought with, had fostered an Iraqi military adequate to the task of containing the remaining threat, but this military was never given the chance to mature. The first Maliki government, while the United States was still present and had influence, gave initial promise of governing adequately. The prime minister allowed the Iraqi Army to be developed and led with some degree of military logic and success. But the second Maliki government, especially after the United States left in 2011, proved to be disastrous for the army and for Iraq.

We had a relatively stable country, an acceptable army and a promising government ... so what went wrong? First, the Arab Spring led us by diverse means into the depths of the Syrian civil war, which produced ISIS. It is drawing a very long bow to blame that civil war on the US invasion of Iraq. An equally valid argument could be that if the United States had not invaded Iraq today, it would look much more like Syria, which is worse by several orders of magnitude than Iraq.

Second, President Obama did not insist on leaving behind a residual force, contrary to all military advice. For this he was roundly criticised, including by Hillary Clinton, who is reported to have said: "We have residual US forces in Germany, in Japan, in Korea to this day, yet after these awful eight years, with 4500 Americans killed and 100,000 to 150,000 Iraqis killed, we're prepared to walk away?" Had there been a residual US force in Iraq, there may not have been an ISIS invasion, and even if there had been, the Iraqi Army probably would not have folded. It is interesting that President Obama has now agreed to leave such a force in Afghanistan, and that his administration is even hinting at extending it.

Third, the second Maliki administration proved to be sectarian, corrupt and incompetent. Maliki replaced army commanders with sectarian cronies who stole the pay of the army in Mosul, made the soldiers buy their ammunition, did not fund army training and equipment and destroyed their morale and trust. No wonder they broke, and that the Maliki-installed commanders led the rout.

Kilcullen's essay was written before the fall of Ramadi in Iraq and Palmyra in Syria, and before the attempts to retake parts of Anbar. His view that we do not yet have the right mix of support for the Iraqis now has added urgency, especially given that the Assad regime is showing signs of cracking. Should Assad fall, ISIS may decide to devote even greater resources to Iraq. We know that ISIS can be defeated militarily in Iraq, if we have the necessary resolve, given what the Kurds are succeeding in doing. Once Iraqi sovereignty is re-established in northern and eastern Iraq, then who knows what might be possible for the Syrian people? But a solution to the Syria problem is far beyond the bounds of feasible planning until we have restored at least a degree of Iraqi sovereignty over the whole of the country.

Like Kilcullen, I am prepared to acknowledge that the invasion of Iraq may not have been a strategically brilliant move. However, there is nothing more stupid than getting yourself into an unnecessary war and then bungling its execution. You can get yourself into the wrong war, but still win. It is not only the grand strategic choice that determines success or failure; it is also how you implement the strategy. Yet our current tepid response runs the risk of seeing Iranian control and influence stretch from the Northern Arabian Gulf to the Mediterranean – true folly indeed.

A Chinese general once said that strategy without tactics is a slow road to victory, but tactics without strategy is noise before defeat. What would he have said of a war in which the strategy is challenged and the tactics are lacking – a slow road to noisy defeat?

When we say that we (Australians) are "training the Iraqis," the uninitiated assume that we are training them to be fully competent for combat. Nothing could be further from the truth. I don't know exactly what training our "advise and assist" force is offering today to an Iraqi brigade, but the training will take at best months and more likely weeks, and our advisers are not accompanying the Iraqis into combat.

Back in 2004–05 in Iraq, Australians conducted as much training as possible in a very short time. The Australians and British did not accompany the Iraqis into battle. You cannot train for experience and leadership in only a few weeks. And you can only develop that on a battlefield while you remain alive.

The United States accompanied the Iraqis they trained into battle, at the early stage with only nine advisers per 500-strong battalion, but later with up to thirty advisers. The US ran a "train – fight – train" sequence to build experience. It was tactically successful because they accompanied the troops they trained into battle, whereas the British and the Australians did not accompany them and were not successful. Non-accompanied units were either intimidated out of existence once they were on their own, or they failed in combat and the troops were killed or deserted, or, as at Basra, were suborned to support the Sadrists.

Both Australia and the United Kingdom implicitly admitted their error in Iraq by accompanying the units they trained into battle in Afghanistan and, on a very long road to vague victory, they were tactically successful. When accompanied, the local soldiers will be paid, intelligence can be brought into the unit, fire support is accessed, and the soldiers receive ammunition, food and fuel. Local commanders make better tactical decisions and don't get their soldiers killed as carelessly. The Iraqi soldiers are not fools. They know that they will not be abandoned – as happened at Mosul – if there are advisers with them. Any veteran of the Australian Army Training Team Vietnam will tell you that.

Kilcullen points out that the greatest tactical tool in Iraq at the moment is air power, but it must be correctly applied. To do this, two changes are needed. First, the rules of engagement must be appropriate to the battlefield. Iraq now is not Afghanistan. Inappropriate rules of engagement are restricting the targets that can be attacked. This is being exploited by ISIS. The strategic price that we are paying is that we are not winning. The law of armed conflict will not be transgressed if there is more freedom in what aircraft can attack. More innocents will be killed, but this must be balanced morally against a much longer road to victory. Tighter rules of engagement do not necessarily deliver a more humanitarian result. They may just prolong the agony.

Second, the effectiveness of airpower will be greatly enhanced if the bombs dropped against certain targets are controlled from the ground by what is called a "joint terminal attack controller" (JTAC). Better targets can be chosen and better results achieved. The tactical ability of even the smallest unit is magnified, as is the confidence of the soldiers on the ground. Terminal control of bombs, even through a sandstorm as at Ramadi, could have delivered a strategic effect.

JTACs need to be protected and supported while they are supporting and protecting units. Thus, we must combine training with accompanying Iraqi units into battle, realistic rules of engagement and the deployment of JTACs. Of course there is a risk of adviser casualties. But there is also a distinct risk of winning without having to put boots on the ground: a strategic imperative. No guarantee, just an increased probability. It is not panic time in Iraq, even though it has not been a good few months. But the longer we do not defeat ISIS decisively within Iraq, the higher the chance of external events which totally dislocate our Iraq operational strategy, and what price any grand strategy then?

We should be acting now to avoid a slow road to noisy defeat. If we are committed, we take responsibility for the outcome. We do not just go through the motions and conduct training. As one of the many great Australian soldiers of the Vietnam era reminded me, the Vietnamese would say, "Either protect us and be with us, or leave us alone." David Kilcullen's essay reminds us that certain lessons are immutable over time: political resolve is essential to victory, and victory is what we should be aiming for.

Jim Molan

Waleed Aly

As I write this, Australia is considering an American request to undertake an expanded military campaign against ISIS in Syria. Actually, let's be more accurate: we're considering our own request, made formally by America after we pushed for it to do so. If that sounds unusual, perhaps the Abbott government's determination – revealed by Laura Tingle – to find a national security announcement every week until the election might help explain it. As you read this, the "decision" has probably been made.

Which doesn't necessarily make it entirely baseless. Truth be told, it never made any sense to confine airstrikes to Iraq. For as long as Australia wasn't asked, it could avoid Syria under American camouflage. But ISIS has completely dissolved the Iraq–Syria border as a matter of practical reality. It exists now only as a political fiction, and Tony Abbott is undoubtedly correct to suggest that our adherence to that fiction can only help ISIS. Indeed, as David Kilcullen has shown, it is precisely this fiction that allowed ISIS to develop in the first place: to regroup in Syria after failure in Iraq, and return as a more hardened and formidable fighting outfit. It remains the case, as Kilcullen notes, that "the Islamic State can always use its sanctuary in Syria to recover from defeat in Iraq."

So we'll go. But what we almost certainly won't do is anything resembling what Kilcullen suggests in *Blood Year*. No "radically increased weight of air power" and certainly no "larger number of ground troops than at present – but under very different rules of engagement." Kilcullen is clearly as sceptical about this as I am, pointing to President Obama's foreign policy instinct to resist anything hawkish that isn't executed by remote control. The other widely acknowledged factor is simply that, for better or worse, we're over this stuff. Western nations are drained of the political will that would see them make a new blood sacrifice. Hence the reflex rejection of "ground troops" in favour of more managerial terms like "advisers."

Never again miss an issue. Subscribe and save.

☐ **1 year subscription** (4 issues) $59 (incl. GST). Subscriptions outside Australia $89.
All prices include postage and handling.

☐ **2 year subscription** (8 issues) $105 (incl. GST). Subscriptions outside Australia $165.
All prices include postage and handling.

☐ Tick here to commence subscription with the current issue.

PAYMENT DETAILS I enclose a cheque/money order made out to Schwartz Publishing Pty Ltd.
Or please debit my credit card (MasterCard, Visa or Amex accepted).

CARD NO. ☐☐☐☐ ☐☐☐☐ ☐☐☐☐ ☐☐☐☐

EXPIRY DATE   /   CCV   AMOUNT $

CARDHOLDER'S NAME

SIGNATURE

NAME

ADDRESS

EMAIL   PHONE

tel: (03) 9486 0288 **fax:** (03) 9486 0244 **email:** subscribe@blackincbooks.com **www.quarterlyessay.com**

An inspired gift. Subscribe a friend.

☐ **1 year subscription** (4 issues) $59 (incl. GST). Subscriptions outside Australia $89.
All prices include postage and handling.

☐ **2 year subscription** (8 issues) $105 (incl. GST). Subscriptions outside Australia $165.
All prices include postage and handling.

☐ Tick here to commence subscription with the current issue.

PAYMENT DETAILS I enclose a cheque/money order made out to Schwartz Publishing Pty Ltd.
Or please debit my credit card (MasterCard, Visa or Amex accepted).

CARD NO. ☐☐☐☐ ☐☐☐☐ ☐☐☐☐ ☐☐☐☐

EXPIRY DATE   /   CCV   AMOUNT $

CARDHOLDER'S NAME   SIGNATURE

NAME

ADDRESS

EMAIL   PHONE

RECIPIENT'S NAME

RECIPIENT'S ADDRESS

tel: (03) 9486 0288 **fax:** (03) 9486 0244 **email:** subscribe@blackincbooks.com **www.quarterlyessay.com**

Delivery Address:
37 LANGRIDGE St
COLLINGWOOD VIC 3066

Quarterly Essay
Reply Paid 79448
COLLINGWOOD VIC 3066

No stamp required
if posted in Australia

Delivery Address:
37 LANGRIDGE St
COLLINGWOOD VIC 3066

Quarterly Essay
Reply Paid 79448
COLLINGWOOD VIC 3066

Our present strategy of airstrikes coupled with training of local groups (including the Iraqi Army) to fight ISIS is only the strategy because we don't really have one. In fact, it is surely the opposite of a strategy, since we've been following it – with an unblemished record of failure – for over a decade. And not just us: NATO, Jordan, South Korea, Romania – even Iran – have attempted the same thing. America blew something in the order of $40 billion trying to train these groups. Then, at the first sign of ISIS, they buckled or fled.

So Kilcullen is plainly right in saying that if we're serious about stopping ISIS – by which he means removing its state-like properties – our "advisers will have to be able to accompany their supported units into battle." But there is something telling about our reason for not doing this. Our inaction is not typically explained as a strategic decision. It is not sold to us as a matter of careful restraint. We aren't withholding ground troops because we feel that our military absence is a prerequisite for success; that our presence is so politically toxic that it will only strengthen ISIS's hand. Rather, the aversion to sacrifice seems to be the point. We're scared of ISIS. We'll talk them up as a "death cult" that is "coming after us." But we're clearly not concerned enough to risk anything serious.

Which is why I had a deeply impolitic thought: what if, for all the huffing and hyperventilating, no one really – *really* – cares about ISIS? Not just us in the West, but anyone in a position to do anything about it. Because we're far from alone in our unwillingness to risk soldiers' lives. The Iraqi military cannot avoid confrontation, but it is perfectly happy for Shi'a militias to carry the load. Those militias, of course, are backed by Iran, but are most often local fighters. Iran is happy to be a patron, but scarcely more. Its clear preference is to keep its military at a distance, with senior officials occasionally touring the frontlines for photo opportunities and morale-boosting. It is the Iraqi Shi'a poor who do the dying.

The reasons for this, it turns out, aren't vastly different from those prevailing in the West: the Iranian people are queasy about sending their own soldiers to die. They don't like ISIS. Like us, they fear them to a point – no doubt more than we do, given their closer proximity to ISIS's lands. But not enough to reconcile them to anything more than a training-and-support strategy in Iraq and Syria – even as it becomes clear that this won't be sufficient. So when Bashar al-Assad admits his army is depleted and has lost territory, and while Iran's Revolutionary Guard chief Qasem Soleimani makes interventionist noises in the wake of a series of Syrian government losses, nothing seems to change. The strategy – for all its lack of success – remains: local militias in Iraq, and Hezbollah in Syria.

But then, success is relative. It is largely a matter of what you're happy to accept. By that measure, perhaps the strategy has succeeded. It's true ISIS continues to exist. But it's also true that the Kurds have recaptured most of the lands they'd lost, and that, for now at least, thanks to the US-led air campaign and the Shi'a militias, ISIS is contained. And then there's life in Baghdad, which, if you believe Nicolas Pelham's recent account in the *New York Review of Books*, is returning to something strangely mundane: "less of a failed state than normally depicted ... uncannily lacking in trauma." Pelham notes the minutiae. Police fining drivers whose paperwork isn't up to scratch. Courts sentencing those who don't pay. People talking about ISIS in the past tense, while young men blast ISIS-mocking pop songs from their car stereos. Bars and nightclubs open. Literary festivals. Museums re-opening and high-school students touring them for the first time in nearly twenty-five years. New trains. Businesspeople investing their money locally. Suicide bombings down to roughly one a week. Normality, I suppose, is relative too.

The north really is another country. The militias provide a degree of security in the south, but they can't penetrate ISIS's northern heartlands. Meanwhile, the Sunnis trapped in ISIS's *régime de la terreur* are rapidly growing to detest their brutal overlords, but might just fear the Shi'a to the south even more. This, as Kilcullen notes, is the consequence of Nouri al-Maliki's disastrously sectarian rule, and it is not easily unwound. All of which raises an obvious question: if life in the south is approaching some version of normal, if ISIS is contained, and if the Sunnis in the north and the Shi'a in the south are so divided and mutually hostile, then why would the Iraqi state bother any longer? Why not say goodbye to the north, and stay resolute in defending the south from any ISIS advance?

To be sure, that outcome would trouble the West. If Baghdad relies on Tehran-backed militias for its security, then the Iraqi state is beholden to Iran. No doubt Iraq's prime minister knows this. But it is less clear how Western intervention of the kind Kilcullen proposes would change that. Perhaps he is right to suggest Iraq would rather have American help than Iranian, but that help is clearly not urgently needed in the south. It would make much more difference in the north, but there the Iranians are hardly competing for influence with unbridled vigour.

A more muscular intervention of the kind Kilcullen advocates would likely prevent Iranian domination of a huge swathe of the region, running from Iran itself right through to Syria. That would no doubt please the Sunni powers like Saudi Arabia and Turkey, as well as Israel and America. But sadly, the politics of the region are never so neat. What, for example, would be the political aftermath? Who would rule the north? Baghdad? The nation formerly known as Iraq is now so deeply rent that any strategy for stronger intervention must surely include a strategy to convince the Sunnis that in spite of everything they've suffered at the hands of the recent Iraqi state, things will be different this time. Maybe Prime

Minister Abadi can win such an argument. But we would want to be confident before intervening, because it's unlikely the Sunnis will be in much of a mood to listen to the same Western forces whose invasion took away the dominance they enjoyed under Saddam Hussein. The perception of American–Shi'a collaboration runs deep in Sunni Iraq. And if the Sunni tribes detest the Shi'a enough to put up with ISIS, they might not think much of us, either.

And this, of course, is to say nothing of Syria, which, by consensus, simply must be solved politically should any response to ISIS be successful. Indeed, Kilcullen has as a condition of his military proposal that Assad agree to a political settlement. That much is utterly essential. But it has thus far also proven to be utterly fanciful. The UN is incapable of enforcing anything, thanks to Russian obstruction, and Assad shows no sign of agreeing to a settlement. In any event, such a settlement would need to identify who would control the Sunni parts of Syria – and with all the Sunni turmoil in the region, who could take on this mantle without immediately being besieged by forces as bad as ISIS?

There may be answers to these questions. And if there are, I'd certainly trust Kilcullen to guide me to them. But call me pessimistic. Pessimistic that the noxious politics of the region, which we helped stir up by invading Iraq, will somehow become less noxious with the application of greater military force. Pessimistic about our capacity to navigate these fault-lines, given the trust and political capital we've shredded so far. Pessimistic because the relatively successful intervention in the Balkans provides no model for a region as wrecked as this one.

Right now, I can imagine a long-term outcome that leaves a reconfigured Middle East: a Shi'a state in southern Iraq, an Alawite one in what remains of Syria, and a contained ISIS no one is particularly desperate to dislodge as long as the atrocities are confined to those unfortunate enough to be ruled by it. Such reconfigurations are always extremely bloody, and this one would leave in its wake two profoundly evil regimes – maybe three, if Iran gets hold of Baghdad. The human cost will be catastrophic. But the world has shown impeccable form when it comes to ignoring such catastrophes. Assad has been banking on it for years.

I'd like to avoid that. So, in my helplessness, I'm open to being convinced on military intervention. To be sure, we've shown we're not terribly good at it in the Middle East. But there is at least the logical possibility that we'll do it well the next time. For that, though, we'll need every question answered. We'll need to show not merely that a desperate situation exists – that we have to do *something* – but also that we're on top of the politics, and that the cure we're offering won't end up worse than the disease.

Waleed Aly

Paul McGeough

In a news report in the *Washington Post* this morning, the United States is described as "the greatest nation in the world." A *Post* op-ed the other day referred to the US as "the leader of the free world," and in the election campaign now under-way you'll see the presidential nominees tested on their allegiance to the doctrine of American exceptionalism.

Amid so much self-congratulatory greatness, how to explain Washington's serial bungling in the Middle East? And in that context, what are we to make of David Kilcullen's recent contribution to the debate?

As an Australian counterinsurgency expert with years of service in the US military and diplomatic machine, Kilcullen is rightly critical of the American record in Afghanistan and Iraq. He had a front-row seat for that, but now he's doubling down, urging all-out war against ISIS – and in so doing, he seems to gloss over the usefulness of the elements of counterinsurgency.

Millions of defenceless citizens are caught up in the mess that is Iraq and Syria. Millions more in the region are destabilised as its impact is felt across the region, or they suffer under regimes that are pampered allies of the West, but which are contemptuous of the rights of their people and also increasingly con-temptuous of their American friends as they run their regional agendas.

Consider: we are in the fifth year of the Syrian crisis, and only recently have Ankara and Washington been able to agree on a no-fly zone to protect thou-sands of Syrian refugees huddling on the Syria–Turkey border. And in the *New York Times* report that broke news of the no-fly zone, we read that a Pentagon program to train and arm rebel fighters in Syria had formally vetted just sixty fighters.

Why so late, so slow, so few? The Middle East is complex, and Syria has to be the most fraught of its serial crises. But Washington and its allies – Australia included – keep going back to the region, assuring us they know how to fix its problems. Remember Tony Abbott's plan for a unilateral Australian invasion of Iraq – 3500 diggers to see off ISIS? Too often, in failing to understand the region, the nature of its conflicts and the resources needed to achieve the stated objectives, the West reveals itself as the problem, not the solution.

Kilcullen knows his stuff, and he's entertaining. But *Blood Year* jars and jolts as he marches on, throwing out Rumsfeldian assurances that this time we know what we're up against, know what we're doing.

He sets up a colossal challenge – then argues that it can be done on a dime. This time, he wants just a conventional military response – no open-ended commitment, no counterinsurgency, none of the counterterrorism effort that cost a fortune in Iraq and Afghanistan and that, with all the drama of a slow-motion car crash, revealed the limits of American power.

Kilcullen figures on foreign combat numbers "moderately larger" than the current 4000 or so. But putting a non-specific division- or corps-sized ceiling on his number means that it could rise to 40,000 on his prescription. He argues that airstrikes, now averaging a paltry 10 a day across both Syria and Iraq, need to be amped up. He's figuring on the scale of Kosovo in 1999 – an average of 250 airstrikes a day over eleven weeks; or the invasion, but not its aftermath, of Afghanistan in 2001 – an initial 5000 troops and about 80 airstrikes a day over ten weeks; or Libya in 2011 – a handful of special operations guys on the ground and 45 airstrikes daily for about seven months.

But in looking at those three interventions, it would be foolhardy to invest all your hopes in a rerun of Kosovo, which ended, militarily, on a relatively tidy note. In both Afghanistan and Libya the aftermath was disastrous – each is still roiled by war and suffering, and Washington rates both as ongoing threats to the national interest. And who can forget the promises that invading Iraq would be "a cakewalk"?

In a war in which more than 200,000 have died in Syria alone, Kilcullen's deference to the counterinsurgency mantra of protecting the population is seemingly limited to taking greater care with airstrikes. Were Rumsfeld, Cheney or Wolfowitz ever so cavalier?

Kilcullen covers himself with this pitch: "This is a case when the job will become much harder, require much more lethal force and do more harm as time goes on: we have to go hard, now, or we'll end up having to go in much harder, and potentially on a much larger scale, later – or accept defeat. The risk is not that ISIS will somehow restart its blitzkrieg and conquer Iraq and Syria. Rather, the threat is that of a regional conflagration if there's no effective international (which, like it or not, means Western-led) response."

But that's all it is – a pitch. He makes no allowance for all that could, and does, go wrong after the first shots are fired in war; or for the so-called Pottery Barn principle, cited by Colin Powell when he prophetically warned George W. Bush as he girded his loins to invade Iraq in 2003: "You are going to be the proud owner of 25 million people. You will own all their hopes, aspirations, and problems. You'll own it all."

In a nutshell, Kilcullen's argument is this: like it or not, the West is already engaged in a conventional military struggle with ISIS, and to get to the other side, it needs to go deeper. Oddly, the voice he quotes at greatest length in his essay is George Mason University's Audrey Kurth Cronin – despite her very different view of the conflict. In the end, he simply disagrees with her, batting back her warnings of the cost of a fully-fledged military campaign, the exhaustion of US resources and the limited chance of success.

In the Middle East, it's as though a history of foreign intervention is sufficient to justify more intervention, as though somehow it's okay to use other people's lives and homelands as laboratories for what might be a smart new Western idea. Merely testing the idea is enough; there is no recognition that by intervening you take on a huge duty of care to the poor buggers whose misfortune it is to live there. Typical of this mindset is former US military and intelligence chief David Petraeus. Co-authoring a "Whither Afghanistan?" piece in the *Washington Post* in June, he wrote: "All is not lost. Far from it. Kabul is much safer than most cities in war zones." But that's a ridiculously low bar when compared to all the lofty reform and development promises – implicit and explicit – made by the West on invading in 2001.

These days, as we read reports of war-weariness driving the US generals to plead for no greater US military involvement in the battle with ISIS, it's as though Kilcullen is channelling the Bush White House – and it's scary. In background briefings to reporters, the generals have become leery, because they don't see a viable outcome. But Kilcullen writes more about what his expansion would not be, than what it would: "I think we should explicitly rule out any occupation and commit only to a moderately larger number of ground troops than at present – but under very different rules of engagement, and with a radically increased weight of air power to back them ... Why so hawkish a response? Because this is an escalating threat that's growing and worsening." And if "we" don't, he warns, there is the risk of a regional implosion.

Some years back, while interviewing Kilcullen, I speculated on what level of insurgency violence would make Iraq ungovernable. In response, he assured me that the level of violence was less important than the capacity of a government to deal with it. By that measure Iraq and Syria have had it, and it could be that the near-century-old borders of the Middle East are dissolving before our eyes. And if the Syria and Iraq imagined by British and French diplomats Sykes and Picot are over, their absence could well call into question the viability of Jordan and Lebanon. Based in Beirut, the former British intelligence agent and diplomat Alastair Crooke goes further, depicting ISIS as a "veritable time bomb inserted in the heart of the Middle East," with all the potential to cause the "implosion of Saudi Arabia as a foundation stone of the modern Middle East." So the risk of conflagration is real and I'm not sure that it is fully understood or appreciated outside the Middle East.

*

Kilcullen is right on Osama bin Laden's masterstroke in aggregating what previously were localised grievances and conflicts to create a global jihad against the West, from Somalia to Indonesia to Chechnya. Addressing a military audience in 2003, Kilcullen noted that, "Without the ... ability to aggregate dozens of conflicts into a broad movement, the global jihad ceases to exist. It becomes simply a series of disparate local conflicts that are capable of being solved by nation-states ... A strategy of Disaggregation would seek to dismantle, or break up, the links that allow the jihad to function as a global entity."

However, there are three problems here. One, the advent of the internet and social media made aggregation a no-brainer for terrorists. Two, bin Laden was able to offer himself as a saviour to those in crisis around the world precisely because the West did little or nothing to address their grievances. And three, how can those "nation-states" be relied on to do anything if they are failing, broken or rife with corruption?

It might well be that no amount of Western intervention will head off an implosion. But in the meantime, there is a way around the seeming resignation in Washington to a choice between anarchy and autocracy. As the Brookings Institution's Shadi Hamid argues, "If ISIS and what will surely be a growing list of imitators are to be defeated, then statehood and, more importantly, states that are inclusive and accountable to their people are essential."

The West is too willing to intervene militarily, and too reluctant to confront autocratic leaders on abuse of the rights of their people. Thus Kilcullen dwells more on support for governments than he does on support for peoples. He acknowledges that on invading Iraq, the West had a "legal and ethical obligation to stabilise the society we'd disrupted." Yet he concludes that Iraq is again sovereign and independent, and hence "no such obligation exists now."

Sovereign and independent. Really? Baghdad and Damascus have each lost control of about one-third of their territory, they don't control their common border and they can neither protect nor provide for their people. Kilcullen then tries to argue that although ISIS-controlled territory overlays both these supposedly sovereign nations, ISIS is itself a state, so it is a legitimate military target for the West. At the same time, Kilcullen rates the Assad regime as "odious," but implies that its dubious sovereignty should somehow protect it from the same fate as Saddam Hussein's regime. Like others, he seems bent on keeping both Iraq and Syria as post-Ottoman, Western constructs, crafted for Western, not local, interests.

*

In the absence of policies that genuinely serve the interests of the peoples of the region, there is an argument that containment is a better option for handling ISIS. It's ungainly and uncertain, to be sure, but it does seem to fit somewhere between Kilcullen's hedged options – at one point he argues that maybe ISIS will mellow, as revolutionary Moscow and Tehran did, and elsewhere that ISIS is irreconcilable and so must be destroyed. Maybe it's time to test a line thrown out there, back in 1923, by one fabled British diplomat to another – Gertrude Bell to Percy Cox. Bell wrote: "I believe that however much we know about the East, what we never can know is the effect orientals will have on one another if you leave them to themselves."

Despite efforts to blame Islam for the mayhem in the region, the problem is in the region's capitals, not in the Koran. More pertinent than "What's wrong with Islam?" is this question: if the Iraqi tribes were willing to see off al-Qaeda in Iraq, why do they acquiesce in the face of this onslaught by ISIS?

Audrey Cronin, writing in the March–April 2015 issue of Foreign Affairs, argued that the old US counterinsurgency drill, in which Kilcullen had a hand, doesn't fit today's conflict, because "the Shiite-dominated Iraqi government has so badly undercut its own political legitimacy that it might be impossible to restore it ... [and] Washington ... cannot lend legitimacy to a government it no longer controls." Kilcullen concedes that local Sunnis see any likely alternative as a worse deal than the one they get under ISIS – especially anything led by the United States. But by invoking Kanan Makiya's Republic of Fear to liken ISIS control to that of Saddam Hussein, Kilcullen misses another point: so many countries in the Middle East are republics of fear, to varying degrees, that fear is a regional norm. Theirs is the stability Hillary Clinton said we had to have in Egypt, as protesters in Cairo chanted "Down, down, Hosni Mubarak" in January 2011; theirs the restoration of democracy for which John Kerry thanks the Egyptian field marshal Abdel Fattah al-Sisi.

Kilcullen does acknowledge that security aid in the absence of government reform, human rights, rule of law, and economic development will backfire. But in dwelling on broad security issues, he diminishes the latter as essential elements in his equation, especially as the Saudis are becoming more aggressive and the United States and others sell more and more arms into the region, despite a near total refusal by the regimes to commit ground forces to fight ISIS.

Later, Kilcullen explains away the White House resort to drone strikes and unilateral Special Forces raids as "tacit recognition that partnerships with local governments were not succeeding." At the same time, he argues that it would take years for alternatives like thoroughgoing anti-corruption and political reform programs to make governments capable of dealing with terrorism. But such programs only have a chance of working *before* the onset of terrorism; once it starts, you've got Buckley's — because the local leaders targeted for Western reform therapy quickly become aware that they are in a position to manipulate their would-be foreign reformers.

Interesting, too, is how Kilcullen casts al-Qaeda in the context of the Arab Spring. As he sees it, the death of Osama bin Laden mired the movement in a protracted leadership struggle. "AQ was absent ... failing [for the moment] to infiltrate the Arab Spring, and the grievances it sought to exploit were being resolved peacefully, which was the last thing it wanted."

I beg to differ. Short-lived as it was, and though so few of the grievances it raised were actually resolved, the Arab Spring was proof of how tens of millions of young and frustrated Arabs, over-educated and under-employed, might have responded to a long-term campaign of social, cultural and educational diplomacy coupled with some severe bullying by the West, instead of the West slobbering over their corrupt leaders. As Condoleezza Rice said in Cairo in the northern summer of 2005, clearly on a day when she had not been drinking the exceptionalist Kool-Aid: "For 60 years, my country, the United States, pursued stability at the expense of democracy in ... the Middle East, and we achieved neither."

For a secretary of state who got it so right in 2005, she got it absurdly wrong the following year, when she described the Israeli invasion of Lebanon as "the birth pangs of a new Middle East." No — that would have been the Arab Spring, when it was the West, potentially far more influential than al-Qaeda is or was, that was missing in action.

Paul McGeough

Audrey Kurth Cronin

Dave Kilcullen and I met in late 2005, when I came to Washington briefly for meetings and he was working at the US Department of State for Ambassador Hank Crumpton, the Counterterrorism Coordinator. In those days I was Director of Studies for the Changing Character of War Programme at Oxford University. In 2006–07, Dave occasionally stopped by Oxford on his way to or from Iraq. We'd test out ideas, debate or brainstorm about counterterrorism – in formal seminars or over beers at a local pub. I greatly respected Dave's insight, dedication and experience. We agreed most of the time, and I always came away enriched.

Not having had the pleasure of his stimulating conversation lately, I read Dave's essay with keen interest. It is a heartfelt piece, written with characteristic acumen. His distress at the 2014 rise of ISIS and effective dismantling of the state of Iraq comes through, as does his personal sense of duty. He argues that for ten years the United States has followed essentially the same counterterrorism strategy, which Dave calls "Disaggregation," and that it has failed. He writes, "I know this strategy intimately, because I helped devise it. So its failure is in part my failure too." I live in Washington now. It's refreshing to hear such clear acceptance of responsibility. Bravo to a man of integrity.

But Dave is assuming too much burden. First, Disaggregation was a brilliant approach, but it was never an overarching logic for all US policy. If only it had been. The purpose of Disaggregation was to keep our enemies divided, manage down the problem and avoid strategic overreach. Thus, it sought to emphasise distinctions between groups, many of whom had local grievances predating al-Qaeda (and now the so-called Islamic State), so as to break connections, highlight in-fighting, confront local groups through local partners, and reduce terrorism to a manageable level. Tactically, we did a lot of those things – not least through the tireless work of Dave and Hank, who travelled all over the world building vital counterterrorism partnerships. But strategically, the "Global War on Terror" prevailed.

From the outset there was a contradiction at the heart of Disaggregation. Especially after the misguided invasion of Iraq, generalisations about the seamless, global jihadist movement predominated in the White House, Congress and even the Department of Defense. One of the things Dave and I debated a decade ago was the wisdom of using the related phrase "global insurgency" (for which he is even better known than Disaggregation) as a unifying strategic concept for the war. I worried that this framing would mash disparate groups together and hand the initiative to the jihadists. The United States would be forced into a reactive mode, compelled to respond directly to jihadists not just where there was an imminent threat or serious risk to our national interests, but *everywhere* — a classic recipe for overstretch. Dave's connotation for the phrase was more nuanced, but in practice "global insurgency" became the opposite of Disaggregation. Beginning under the Bush administration and even more so under Obama, the United States built up Special Operations and CIA paramilitary forces, engaging directly in a shadow campaign against this "global insurgency," frequently without the knowledge of local partners.

In his essay, Dave argues that two factors undermined Disaggregation, and that but for these two problems it might have worked. "The first," he writes, "was Iraq." He calls the 2003 invasion of Iraq "the greatest strategic screw-up since Hitler's invasion of Russia" and argues it became "a hole in the heart of Western strategy: the cost, in human life, credibility, money and time, of extracting ourselves from the unforced error weakened the impact of Disaggregation."

Dave is right about the blunder of invading Iraq. There was widespread opposition to the invasion at the time, including from eminent Americans such as former national security advisor Brent Scowcroft, retired marine general Anthony Zinni, and former chairman of the Joint Chiefs of Staff William Crowe. Especially as Iraq became increasingly violent, the occupation sucked up US defence and foreign policy resources, distracting us from what we should have been doing in Afghanistan, Pakistan and elsewhere.

I'm confused about the order of things here. The invasion of Iraq (in 2003) occurred more than two years before, according to Dave, Disaggregation became central to Western strategy (after 2005). Those of us pleading in 2002 that the invasion was a boneheaded counterterrorism move, that it would unite our enemies and alter the regional balance in favour of Iran, were basically stuck with it afterwards. A strategy must take current facts into account and proceed from there.

Having argued that Iraq undermined Disaggregation, Dave contends that we ended the occupation too soon: "you either leave well, or you leave quickly."

Perhaps the US occupation should have gone on longer: I didn't take part in the status of forces agreement (SOFA) negotiations and cannot judge whether the Americans or the Iraqis bear the greater responsibility for precisely when and how the occupation ended.

But it was not "quick." That's a false dichotomy. If anything, we left slowly and badly. The occupation lasted almost nine years, and the costs were terrible. Almost 4500 Americans and an estimated 100,000 Iraqis died. Conservatively, it cost the United States about US$815 billion in direct costs, and a lot more if you include indirect costs (such as support for injured service members and interest on the debt). To put this into perspective, according to World Bank figures, that's more than the annual GDP of most countries (all but seventeen countries have a GDP less than $815 billion). Indeed, it's more than half the annual GDP of Australia. Remember, the Bush administration's original request for war funding was US$21 billion, on the promise that the cost of rebuilding Iraq would be mainly borne by grateful Iraqis. That didn't happen. We will be paying these costs for decades, some of them forever. Ultimately the occupation ended because the willingness of the American people to continue to support the costs of the war had ended.

It didn't take long for simmering sectarian tensions in Iraq to re-emerge. Less than twenty-four hours after the United States pulled out of Iraq, the Shi'a-dominated Maliki government went after its Sunni rivals, methodically removing all trace of Sunni power and influence. Defying a 2008 statute, Maliki developed a federal police force with powers greatly exceeding those of local police. Death squads hunted down prominent Sunnis, killing them or forcing them into exile. Set off by threats of arrest against Finance Minister Rafia al-Issawi, tens of thousands of Iraqi Sunnis came out in peaceful protests in 2012 and 2013. The Shi'a-dominated Iraqi government crushed them, killing at least forty unarmed protesters.

Dave argues that the Maliki government crushed Iraqi Sunnis because the United States had lost its leverage through lack of presidential engagement, the drawdown of troops, spending cuts and a flawed SOFA. "Maliki may have been acting defensively, protecting himself against threats from the military and the Sunnis as American influence waned. But his measures looked offensive to Sunnis, who began to protect themselves against the risk of Shi'a oppression." At what point is a sovereign government responsible for its own policies?

The second factor Dave argues undermined Disaggregation was transformation of the Arab region, triggered by three events: "the death of bin Laden, the failure of the Arab Spring and the rebirth of ISIS." Within that political tsunami, the bloody Syrian civil war both attracted and created Islamist extremists, who joined the most successful anti-Assad faction and gained power, leading directly to the military conquest of ISIS.

When ISIS swept across Iraq in summer 2014, most US military analysts predicted that the US-trained Iraqi security forces would contain it. The United States had spent US$26 billion on the Iraqi security forces alone during almost a decade of occupation. Iraq should have had an army able to turn back the advance of ISIS and a police force willing and able to protect the rights and interests of the Sunni minority. It did not.

Instead, the advance was met with mass desertions from the Iraqi Army. With the Maliki government carrying out brutal sectarian policies, the Sunnis had nowhere else to turn. Secular Iraqi military officers and Iraqi Sunni tribal leaders who had formerly been aligned with the 2006 "Surge" abandoned the Iraqi state and aligned themselves with ISIS. Now ISIS's military operations are led by capable former Iraqi military leaders who know US techniques and have US-supplied equipment, including American tanks, artillery, armoured humvees and mine-resistant vehicles.

The rise of ISIS and the establishment of the "Islamic State" has been disastrous for Iraq, which no longer functions as a nation-state. Many indigenous Iraqis have fled, resulting in the worst displacement crisis since World War II. Meanwhile, some 1000 foreign fighters a month, including fighters from the United Kingdom, the United States, Europe and Australia, have flocked to the Islamic State. And ISIS has developed global, 24-hour online operations and a cadre of trained social media recruiters, who draw vulnerable teenagers and disaffected Muslims to the "caliphate" or goad them to carry out terrorist attacks against "infidels" at home.

The Islamic State will be defeated, but not directly by the democratic powers using their own conventional forces. A core part of the myth of the Islamic State is its claim to be a caliphate. If we flood the region with troops, we will supply the pretext for the theological nonsense its spokespeople spout. They tell their followers the caliphate will soon face what they call the army of "Rome," meaning Christian-majority states, who will confront them in towns like Dabiq in northern Syria and initiate a countdown to the apocalypse. It would be foolish to play into that narrative. They would use it to mobilise or inspire additional supporters in the region, and the threat of homegrown attacks would grow.

But that does not mean we should be passive. We must attack this threat with sustainable policies that can achieve our political objectives. These include bearing down with punishing airstrikes on ISIS targets, supporting the Iraqis and the

Kurds as they fight, continuing arms embargos and sanctions, and choking off ISIS smuggling routes. While containing them militarily, we should greatly increase aid to civilians fleeing the fighting. Moreover, we must recognise that ISIS is not merely an American or Western coalition problem. The wars in Iraq and Syria involve not only regional players but also major global actors such as Russia, Turkey, Iran, and Saudi Arabia and other Gulf states. Dave fears that regional and world powers will be drawn in; I argue that they are already there.

The United States cannot single-handedly defend the region and the world from an aggressive, revisionist, theocratic state – nor should it. The major powers must develop a common diplomatic, economic and military approach to ensure that this pseudo-state is tightly contained and treated as a global pariah. In short, we should "aggregate." The good news is that no government supports ISIS. It is an enemy of every state in the region – and indeed the world. To capitalise on this, Washington and its allies should pursue a more aggressive diplomatic agenda with major powers and regional players. NATO's declaration of support for Turkey's anti-ISIS campaign is a step in the right direction.

Dave ends his essay maintaining that the most important thing is "the centrality of political will." I agree. But in Iraq, the political will of Western societies is secondary to the political will of the Iraqis. I sincerely hope that the new Iraqi government will be able to rally its inhabitants – Shi'a and Sunni alike – to support and fight for it, especially with the help of aggressive American and Australian air power. But no matter how much equipment or how many embedded advisers we provide, external powers will never be able to force them to do so. War is, and always has been, a matter of clashing wills.

Audrey Kurth Cronin

Martin Chulov

Having been central to US counterterrorism strategy in the second administration of George W. Bush, David Kilcullen is uniquely placed to discuss its legacy.

From 2004 to 2009, no Australian citizen was closer than Kilcullen to the heart of US strategic decision-making in Iraq, Afghanistan, South Asia and the Horn of Africa. That time at the coalface, as well as his stand-back reflection since, has helped shape his Quarterly Essay *Blood Year*, perhaps one of the most important contributions yet to the global debate on how to deal with what's left behind.

There's much to agree with in Kilcullen's analysis of how the ISIS juggernaut rose to be the existential threat to the post-Ottoman state system that it so clearly is today. Few could dispute his characterisation of events from 2005 to 2009, in particular how the obstinacy of senior officials played a lead role in Iraq's disintegration and how US disengagement gradually emboldened the sectarian agenda prosecuted with such disastrous effect by Nouri al-Maliki.

I would add to this litany a profound cultural ignorance that failed to see how difficult it would be for societies rooted in thousands of years of tribal custom to embrace a new way of life that values individual liberties above all else. And a strategic blindness to how US detention centres were to become incubators in which ISIS would organise and plot. Without facilities such as Camp Bucca, ISIS leaders would not now pose the same threat.

Kilcullen's conclusion — that deeper military re-engagement with committed local partners is the only short-term way to slow ISIS's momentum — also stands to reason. But he, along with everyone else in the global policy sphere, is yet to come up with an approach about what to do beyond a containment plan.

The region is more combustible than at any time in the past century. The Sunni/Shi'a showdown now rumbling through the heart of Arabia eclipses in significance some rather notable events along the way: the creation of Israel in 1948,

Iran's Islamic Revolution in 1979, the decade of war with Iraq that followed, and two US wars against Saddam Hussein.

The region's two biggest power players, Iran and Saudi Arabia, have been engaged in a battle for absolute power for the last five years and show no inclination to compromise. Nor are they likely to as Syria, Lebanon, Yemen and Iraq, where it all began, continue to crumble.

State control in all of these countries is now a facade. Non-state actors have primacy over national institutions in all cases. In Lebanon, the militia cum political bloc Hezbollah runs the show. In Iraq, Shi'a militia groups – all backed by Iran – are more powerful than the country's military. In Syria, it's the same story. ISIS has rendered the border between Iraq and Syria irrelevant.

A root cause of this is ISIS's ability to tap into two narratives, each of which resonates with the region's Sunnis. The jihadi group has been busily riding a suppression narrative on one hand, and a line that Iran has been ascendant at their expense since Saddam was toppled on the other.

The belief is that Sunni disenfranchisement started with the ousting of Saddam, a Sunni strongman in a land of majority Shi'as. It was then advanced by the killing of the patron of Lebanon's Sunnis, Rafiq Hariri, two years later – an assassination blamed on Hezbollah. Disempowerment was then consolidated by the failure of the West to support the Syrian opposition in any meaningful way, so the view goes.

The US nuclear deal with Iran earlier this year has sealed the argument, in the eyes of many Sunnis, as it has with Washington's long-standing Sunni allies in the region, who refuse to accept Obama's claim that such a pact will keep everyone safer in the long run.

The bottom line is that with the regional body politic having so spectacularly failed, ISIS has been able to position itself as a political alternative, which can advance the interests of the majority Muslim sect. In doing so, it can claim to be restoring lost dignity as well as offering safety in numbers to those over whom it lords.

A large part of ISIS's constituency is made up of people who have accepted at least part of this narrative, in the absence of anything else to cling to. Most do not buy into the ISIS ideology but see the group as a bus to a destination – wherever that might be.

If there is to be a way out of this diabolical mess, this group – the Sunnis of Iraq, Syria and Lebanon – need to be given genuine power in an inclusive political process: precisely the formula that was shattered by Maliki as the US left Iraq. With trust so eroded, it is very difficult to see how this could happen. At a local level, there is perhaps a glimmer of residual hope.

In the election of 2010, the bloc of Ayad Allawi, a secular Shi'a, won more seats in Iraq's parliament than Maliki (91 to 89), with much of his support coming from Sunnis. He could not, however, build a coalition that gave him the numbers to form a government. The United States backed Maliki, turning a blind eye to his sectarian ways, and the rest is history.

More broadly, if Humpty Dumpty is ever to be put back together, it will need more than all the king's horses and men. Nothing short of a grand bargain, bringing in all the region's stakeholders – Saudi Arabia, Iran, Turkey, Russia and the United States – is likely to generate real traction. All will need to recognise that mutually assured destruction awaits the region if a power-sharing compromise is not struck.

To the extent that Obama has had a strategy, it has been about the nuclear deal – a good-faith test that could develop into a broader neighbourly role. So far, that has been an impossible sell to Saudi Arabia. And even a full-blown existential crisis may not change that.

One final observation I would like to make on Kilcullen's excellent essay is that by the time Obama entered the White House, he could not have forced an extension of the US presence in Iraq even if he had wanted to. Maliki formed his government in late 2010 with Iran's endorsement, after a pact brokered by the head of the Iranian Revolutionary Guards Quds Force, Qasem Soleimani, and endorsed by Hezbollah's Hassan Nasrallah, Syria's Bashar al-Assad and Muqtada al-Sadr in Iraq.

The condition of the backing was that not a single US remain outside Baghdad's Green Zone. For the United States to stay, Obama would practically have had to reinvade. One insider present at the video conference that sealed the US exit told me that the scenes on each end of the link that day could not have been more different. In the White House situation room sat a phalanx of generals, along with Obama, Joe Biden, Hillary Clinton and others. In Baghdad, Maliki sat with an empty notebook and a translator. The discussion that ended Iraq as it then was took less than five minutes.

Martin Chulov

James Brown

I left Baghdad seven years ago, but the city *Blood Year* takes me back to seems more distant than the moon. How quick and easy to forget the desperate reality of everyday life in that place – a city in which dumped children, "eyes gouged out, ears, little limbs and genitals hacked off," are the literal embodiment of cruel political calculus. In which the needs of al-Qaeda in Iraq prompted a macabre secondary market to procure kidnapped children to be dumped.

Once again, David Kilcullen has become our avatar navigating that nether-world, forcing us to negotiate our own sensibilities in order to understand the rationale that drives the Islamic State. It's no easy task: he punctuates an Austral-ian political debate on terrorism dumbed down by prime ministerial invocations of the death cult and its deranged diaspora of foreign fighters and remotely rad-icalised youth.

For all the talk of Australia's political and security leaders in the year since Mosul fell, little insight has been provided into the motivations of ISIS. Kilcul-len's essay sheds much-needed light on its origins, tracing its lineage from both Iraq and al-Qaeda and explaining its resurgence through the sanctuary provided by a chaotic Syrian civil war. ISIS's leaders are focused on their own political survival first and foremost, Kilcullen reminds us, and willing to commit atroci-ties against their own people if that's what it takes to solidify and strengthen their position. But these are not capricious barbarians: al-Baghdadi himself is a scholar – he and his followers were schooled through the terrorist universities that US prisons like Camp Bucca became.

By any measure Islamic State has been wildly successful, sometimes in spite of its own strategies, policies and military tactics. As Kilcullen notes, it is now a state-like entity, controlling more territory than Israel and with a larger popula-tion than New Zealand. This success, I suspect, has surprised even the most committed of ISIS commanders. A senior military commander within Islamic

State interviewed last year concluded that their campaign "got bigger than any of us. This can't be stopped now. This is out of the control of any man. Not Baghdadi, or anyone else in his circle." An anonymous NATO official writing in the *New York Review of Books* conceded glumly in August that "Nothing since the triumph of the Vandals in Roman North Africa has seemed so sudden, incomprehensible, and difficult to reverse as the rise of ISIS. None of our analysts, soldiers, diplomats, intelligence officers, politicians, or journalists has yet produced an explanation rich enough – even in hindsight – to have predicted the movement's rise." Islamic State has become a viral political campaign, fuelled by actual and perceived conventional military victories.

The IRA had Gerry Adams to carry forth its message, drive recruitment and secure funding from the diaspora. ISIS has tens of thousands of Twitter accounts, professionally produced snuff films and communications experts producing a stream of media missives. (Our political leaders should be able to understand this campaign better than most.) And here, I think, is the fertile ground on which the counterstrategy against ISIS will be found. I agree with Kilcullen that the United States and its allies and partners (both in the West and the Middle East) could do more to contain the advance of ISIS on the ground (although I don't necessarily think that this translates to a larger role for the Australian Defence Force). It is far more difficult to contain ISIS in the arena of public perception.

But countering the ISIS narrative is not impossible. The group's need to stay connected is its vulnerability. In June, coalition aircraft destroyed an ISIS command-and-control building after a foreign fighter accidentally provided the building's coordinates in a boastful selfie posted to Twitter. And Islamic State's politico-media operatives can be targeted in Special Forces operations in the same way. Like any Western political party, ISIS values leaders who can shape their political communications campaigns. Such skills are in shorter supply than the ability to operate heavy weapons and manage fighters on the battlefield. Attrite enough of Islamic State's media commanders (the nodes in their political communications networks) and we will start to see the group's momentum falter. Consider, for example, the impact on Columbia's FARC movement after its spokesman was killed in 2008.

Destroying the ISIS narrative does need actual tactical wins on the ground, and they are in short supply at the moment. US Secretary of Defense Ashton Carter was scathing in his assessment of the Iraqi Security Forces in Ramadi, who "vastly outnumbered the opposing force, and yet they failed to fight." That's not to say the Iraqis have lost all will to fight – ISIS recently executed several of its commanders for fleeing Iraqi security forces tenaciously defending the Baiji oil refinery. But the campaign to re-take Mosul is some way off and efforts to re-train the Iraqi Army look to be a matter of years, not months.

Australia has not even begun its national effort in the battle of ideas – the counter-messaging war. The statements of our political leaders remain stilted; efforts to engage Muslim communities have too often been haphazard and hasty. An $18-million centre for counter-narratives is still just an announcement. The real question is why this critical component of the fight has received such limited funding. If it was worth spending $3 million to advertise the Australian government's Intergenerational Report, surely it is worth spending much more than $18 million on a campaign to destroy a threat the foreign minister judges to be the most challenging for Australia since the Cold War. This is an effort on which our best advertising agencies and our brightest scholars should be engaged. And as Kilcullen rightly points out, it will need to be a continuous campaign in a world of persistent conflict.

The most important contribution of *Blood Year*, though, is to the debate on the balance between national security and freedom currently underway in Australia, thanks to the misguided attempts to strip citizenship rights without trial from those the immigration minister suspects of having been involved with ISIS. Kilcullen identifies the impossible task that voters set for leaders – guarantee us perfect safety from terrorism, but within the constraints of a liberal democracy governed by the rule of law. Little has changed in this regard since the attacks in New York of 2001. Governments cannot inoculate us against every ill, nor stop every terrorist madly committed to the destruction of an Australian target. But our rule of law is precious, worth defending, and even worth risking our lives for. Someday the seemingly unstoppable momentum of ISIS will abate. We must be careful that we don't spend too much of what we truly value in order to bring ISIS down.

James Brown

Clive Kessler

Grounded – might one even say "embedded"? – within a compelling personal narrative is David Kilcullen's acute analytical account of two momentous developments: the collapse of post-Saddam Iraq, despite the brief and surprising hopes of something better that the Bush/Petraeus "Surge" of 2007 briefly offered, and the rise of the so-called caliphate or Islamic State.

That account is set within and cast under the impact of the moment of its own writing: the fateful northern summer of 2014, which witnessed the start of ISIS's territory-grabbing blitzkrieg and, however deformed the product, its ensuing state-building exercise; and also the more distant ramifications of America's "hoping for the best" strategy in Crimea and the Ukraine and the Obama administration's unprofitable, perhaps misguided, nuclear negotiations with Iran.

That is the broader context. But the focus is upon Iraq and ISIS and their intimate causal connection. Upon the emergence and then astounding political momentum of ISIS, a monster of Ba'athist lineage with a grim jihadi visage. No Iraq debacle, no ISIS, or so Kilcullen in effect argues. Hence his primary focus upon Iraq, upon "what went wrong."

What went wrong, Kilcullen argues, is three things. First, the invasion of Iraq, and the ensuing "de-Ba'athification" of the state and its armed forces under Ambassador Bremer, was a totally misconceived exercise, a losing game. Second, while Iraq became "the main game" – and, so far as geostrategic issues were concerned, the "only game in town" in political Washington – all other Middle East questions were eclipsed. Third was the premature abandoning of the Bush/ Petraeus "Surge" strategy, after its initially improbable successes, by Barack Obama, with his eagerness to "end the war" and "get the troops back home."

The challenge of rescuing and shoring up Iraq is central to Kilcullen's analysis. That is what getting out well, and decently, has to mean: leaving behind an Iraq that was not doomed to immediate collapse once US and allied forces withdrew.

But saying this focuses attention on the question: was this ever possible? Was Iraq itself ever, from the outset, a feasible project? And if it was not, can it be saved?

The oft-repeated cliché, as we mark the centenary of the Great War, is that we are still living, often in very imperfect awareness of this, with its enduring consequences. Iraq is a case in point. As we look at, or flinch from seeing, the daily violence there, we fail to recognise the historical source, and hence also the true nature, of the crisis of the Iraqi state and the agony of its people.

When President Woodrow Wilson brought the United States into World War I on the basis of his "Fourteen Points," he pronounced, with the high-minded insight of a former professor of history, that the only way to end war was to create a world in which the world's national communities might enjoy sovereignty. A world order of nation-states enlisted within a League of Nations.

That principle was upheld and implemented in parts of Europe, but respect for the principle of the self-determination of old "national" communities was less consistently applied in the lands of the former Ottoman Empire.

Britain had made a deal with the sharif of Mecca. It would support, under T.E. Lawrence's plans, Arab nationalism in order to shatter Ottoman domination of the Levant. But the story did not work out well. After the Palestine mandate was declared in 1920, its greater eastern part was severed from it in 1922 by that great political romantic Winston Churchill to become the Emirate of Transjordan under the sharif's son, King (or Emir) Abdullah.

A third son, Faisal, it was hoped, would similarly become the king of Syria. But efforts to impose him there failed, in great part because, under secret wartime agreements (the so-called Sykes–Picot Agreement), Britain had recognised Lebanon and Syria as falling within France's "sphere of influence."

What then to do with Faisal? A brilliant idea! As a Sunni notable he could be installed as king of the Sunni heartland of what was still generally known as Mesopotamia, "the land between the two rivers." That terrain could be put together with the Shi'a areas to the south, centred upon Basra, and the ensuing arrangement would be balanced by the inclusion of the northern Kurdish areas, all within a new state, the Kingdom of Iraq.

The new state was not easily created. When the time came for its birth, via the adoption of its constitution by a constituent assembly of notables, members had to be marched in at gunpoint by the British to vote for it. Not an auspicious start.

The new kingdom did not enjoy a happy history. Always an arena for foreign intrigue and interference, it never knew any stability. Its story ended very badly, and bloodily, with the violent removal of Faisal's grandson, King Faisal II, and his family, together with his prime minister, Nuri al-Said, in 1958. With their gory end, the journey was begun to vindictive Ba'ath Party rule, the reign of its most malign son, Saddam Hussein, and now a horrendous decade of post-Saddam mayhem and collapse.

We are now asked to contemplate with horror the prospect that Iraq may not survive as a unitary state. What is so terrible, one must ask, about that outcome? What great political strength, and what claims to coherent historical identity and recognition, did the Iraqi state ever have? By what logic must it be preserved and its self-devouring agonies be prolonged? Will the world be worse off, and hugely deprived, if we cease insisting that an artificial, quite cynically created entity must be kept alive unnaturally, by extraordinary, and extraordinarily costly, means?

And what is more, if the establishment of a militant new caliphate centred within the borderlands of western Iraq and north-eastern Syria is to be effectively resisted, that will only be done not by an imploding Iraqi state but by the main-stream orthodox Sunnis of the region, acting under their own leadership, defending their own historical zone, or patch of turf and sand, within what was formerly called Mesopotamia.

David Kilcullen wants a genuinely national government in charge of a func-tioning, sustainable Iraqi state to be established, and urges that its Western allies support its military and political consolidation. But that may be too much to ask, a quite unreasonable and unrealistic expectation. Barack Obama has now sent back some additional military advisers and support, and our own prime minister in early June 2015 added his voice to the rallying cry. But will it work? Was it ever on the cards? Can Iraq still hold together? Can its present government hold it together? You would not want to bet on it.

We shall perhaps need to begin doing our hard thinking about what is to hap-pen in the Middle East without the quaint notion of "Iraq." What was it that Bismarck said about Italy? That it was a purely geographical concept, lacking any political reality and substance? Well, very unkind, he was, to Italy. And wrong. But as a summary verdict on Iraq, those words are not far from the mark.

Iraq? It's time for a "three-state solution." Much delayed, it is now long overdue.

*

Iraq may be beyond us, but what are we to do here at home? Some think that we may and should place our trust in the strategy and techniques of "de-radicalisation." There is not much benefit to be had from that quarter, I suspect.

If (and even with quite lavish government support) people want to apply "the social casework approach" piecemeal, at the individual level, and on a patheti-cally Lilliputian scale, to major and deep political and civilisational problems, well, let them try. It may even do a little good, and may not do much harm.

What does do serious harm is to pretend that this kind of approach represents and offers an adequate response to the challenge of militant Islam and Islamism and its radicalising potential.

This threat, the challenge that we now face, is a confrontation of deep historical, religious, cultural and civilisational dimensions. It is folly to pretend otherwise. Militant Islam draws upon powerful doctrinal sources within the Islamic faith and the historical community of Islam. It is not some "disownable" deviant aberration from which the radical young may be weaned or persuaded away or neatly detached by recourse to high-tech gimmickry ("cool" phone apps for confused Muslim youth and the like) and the helping professions' "patter and chatter."

The immediate, practical problem that we face is this: the rest of us cannot resolve this problem for, or without a major effort from, our Muslim fellow citizens. But as things stand, the task cannot be left to them alone, nor is it for them alone to lead – and especially not via simplistic casework tinkering with low-level symptoms and details – on the dubious grounds that "it is their narrative, they own it and they know it best" and similar evasions.

Our Muslim fellow citizens will only be able to play their necessary role – and the rest of us will only be able to support them and their efforts – when a significant transformation has begun; or, at least, when the urgent need for one is recognised within the local (and global) Muslim faith community: in its mind and soul and historical self-understanding.

We need to have a thoughtful, patient, honest and far-reaching conversation about these issues: publicly, and not just in sheltered and cloistered conclaves of community-selected activists, representatives and their chosen interlocutors – while everybody else must remain silent and publicly unheard, on the dubious and insulting grounds of being dangerously infected with "Islamophobia."

This kind of conversation and engagement is the only basis upon which Australia can hope to cope with the fateful challenge that Kilcullen identifies: the challenge of countering the new post-2001 "normal" of "global violence, this convergence of war and crime, of international threats, this rise of a new aggressive totalitarian state from the rubble of the last war" without "surrendering our civil liberties or betraying our ethics." To do this, as Kilcullen recognises, great public will is necessary. But the will that is required is not just political and strategic will of the conventional kind. No less important, and perhaps more fundamental, is the civic will and determination, and also the good sense, of everyday citizens committed in great number to the overarching public good.

Clive Kessler

David Kilcullen

I was honoured to receive such thought-provoking responses to *Blood Year*, from such distinguished commentators. As the range of reactions makes clear, ISIS is a fast-moving subject on which well-intentioned and well-informed people disagree – and which clearly provokes strong emotions.

Indeed, the broader public response to the essay was so strong that I'm now expanding it into a full-length book, which will offer a more detailed treatment of both the history and the issues, including those raised by the correspondents. That book is planned for early 2016, but in the interim I want to offer an update on developments since I finished the essay in April, and to address a few of the respondents' points, focusing on areas where I can offer a factual comment based on current field data (rather than just a personal opinion).

Jim Molan writes:

> Kilcullen's essay was written before the fall of Ramadi in Iraq and Palmyra in Syria, and before the attempts to retake parts of Anbar. His view that we do not yet have the right mix of support for the Iraqis now has added urgency, especially given that the Assad regime is showing signs of cracking. Should Assad fall, ISIS may decide to devote even greater resources to Iraq. We know that ISIS can be defeated militarily in Iraq, if we have the necessary resolve, given what the Kurds are succeeding in doing. Once Iraqi sovereignty is re-established in northern and eastern Iraq, then who knows what might be possible for the Syrian people? But a solution to the Syria problem is far beyond the bounds of feasible planning until we have restored at least a degree of Iraqi sovereignty over the whole of the country.

General Molan is, of course, correct about the pace of events. In fact, things are so dynamic that the combat picture has changed even since his comment was written, and will doubtless shift again by the time this correspondence is published. Beyond the battles he mentions, there have been four huge strategic developments: the Iranian nuclear deal, the entry of Turkey into the war, the Syrian regime's losses over the northern summer of 2015, and the ongoing Iraqi political crisis.

The Iranian deal (formally, the Joint Comprehensive Plan of Action) is still going through a contentious approval process in Washington and Tehran. But it's already having an effect in Syria. Iranian leaders have backed Bashar al-Assad throughout the civil war, offering assistance directly and through proxies like Hezbollah. Until recently, US diplomats have told me, American negotiators were wary of engaging Iranian delegates on Syria, lest doing so increase Tehran's bargaining power in the nuclear talks. Now, with the deal in place, an Iran-backed peace proposal is making its way through the United Nations, Iranian foreign minister Javad Zarif and Quds Force leader Qasem Soleimani have travelled to Russia for consultations, and Washington and Moscow have launched a discreet effort to reopen stalled negotiations on a peaceful settlement of the conflict. This suggests that General Molan's notion that a settlement in Syria will have to wait until ISIS is defeated in Iraq (also the received wisdom at the Pentagon and US Central Command) may be starting to shift. But his broader point stands: regional powers can't contain ISIS – let alone stabilise Iraq or Syria – without a substantially increased and differently targeted effort from the international community to help them make peace where they can, and fight more effectively where they must.

The second major development, and one that underlines the inability of regional powers to contain ISIS on their own, is Turkey's entry into the war. Following ISIS suicide bombings on its territory, Ankara is now letting US combat aircraft strike ISIS in Syria and Iraq from Turkish bases, opening the possibility of a civilian safe zone inside northern Syria, something peace activists and refugee advocates have been demanding for years. This holds potential to reduce the horrendous suffering of Syria's population (and, by extension, to relieve Europe's crisis in dealing with an unprecedented flow of refugees, many of whom are Iraqi or Syrian), provided it's in place before winter comes. The current effort is directed at pushing ISIS away from the Turkish–Syrian border, and Turkey's armed forces have already become involved to a limited extent. All this increases pressure on ISIS, but Turkey has also used it as cover for a renewed offensive against Kurdish separatists, including the PKK. This is understandable, since Turkish leaders fundamentally oppose Kurdish nationalism and detest the Assad regime at least as much as they dislike ISIS, but it runs the risk of undermining any benefit from Turkey's involvement in the conflict. The Kurds, including groups aligned with the PKK, have been critical in holding the line against ISIS in both Iraq and Syria, and the distraction of a Turkish offensive can only disrupt this effort.

Meanwhile, in Syria, the Assad regime lost significant ground over the summer to ISIS, as well as to US-backed rebels operating from the south, and to a joint "operations room" — an alliance of several rebel groups — in the Al-Ghab plain, threatening the critical Mediterranean port city of Latakia and the Alawite mountains, both of which are key bases of government support. The seizure of Palmyra was also a huge blow for the regime, giving ISIS control of more than 50 per cent of Syrian territory. Protests spiked in Syrian cities, increasing pressure on the government, and President Assad is now looking more likely to accept a negotiated settlement — especially since an increasing number of Syrians now see a negotiated peace as the only alternative to collapse and a bloodbath at the hands of ISIS. One Syrian activist told me that a consensus is emerging among opposition groups that "Assad needs to go — his family and his cronies need to leave — but the regime needs to stay, under a provisional or transitional government, or there will be a massacre here." Combined with the "concert of powers" proposals emerging from the Iranian nuclear deal, this suggests that the chances of restarting negotiations toward a Syrian peace are better than they've been for a long time.

Finally, in Iraq, the failure to retake areas ISIS captured in 2014 — along with the humiliating loss of Ramadi, capital of Anbar province, in May 2015 — prompted a political crisis that has rocked the country, leaving Haider al-Abadi's government embattled politically as well as militarily. Former prime minister Nouri al-Maliki (who became one of Iraq's two vice-presidents after he was replaced as PM by Abadi in August 2014) has played an extremely destabilising role. He has aligned with Shi'a-supremacist militias, has sought to bring Abadi down, and is undermining his successor's efforts to address corruption and create a more inclusive political system. The sectarianism, self-serving venality and fecklessness of many (though by no means all) players in Iraq's political elite make it highly unlikely that Sunnis, Kurds or even many Shi'a groups will support Baghdad's efforts against ISIS under these circumstances.

Meanwhile, the Shi'a militias' successes — although these are limited gains that only look good next to the Army's failures — have emboldened Maliki, the militias, sectarian leaders like Muqtada al-Sadr, and Hadi al-Ameri (head of the powerful Iranian-backed paramilitary Badr Organization). Nationwide protests roiled Iraq in August, driven by rage over the government's failure to ensure reliable water and electricity supplies during a heatwave, and triggering a show-down between Maliki and Abadi, as the prime minister sought to abolish the vice-presidency as part of a wider anti-corruption drive. The risk is that Iraqi politicians will squander any remaining legitimacy for civil government – including in the Shi'a-majority south – even as the country experiences a soft military takeover by Iranian-sponsored paramilitaries. Even if that can be avoided, the political basis for an offensive against ISIS – setting aside the daunting military challenges of such an effort – is lacking. Any effort to recapture Ramadi (let alone Mosul) is still some way off, and even in its Shi'a heartland the Baghdad government's writ is increasingly questioned.

All this puts Clive Kessler's comment in perspective. Professor Kessler writes: "We are now asked to contemplate with horror the prospect that Iraq may not survive as a unitary state. What is so terrible, one must ask, about that outcome? … Will the world be worse off, and hugely deprived, if we cease insisting that an artificial, and quite cynically created, entity must be kept alive unnaturally, by extraordinary and extraordinarily costly, means?"

Iraq – as, in fact, I argued in the essay – is already well past the point where it could be considered a unitary state. As I also suggested, it's probably impossible to put it back together. But insouciantly accepting Iraq's break-up would be a terrible idea, for three reasons. First, most importantly, state collapse would trigger a horrific human catastrophe. States engaged in civil wars don't just peacefully break up. Syria has now suffered 250,000 killed (including more than 10,000 children), 12 million displaced and another 12.5 million utterly dependent on humanitarian assistance – an indicator of what would follow a collapse in Iraq. Add in the fact that Iraq's population is 50 per cent larger than Syria's (34 versus 22 million), that ISIS has an agenda so extreme that even al-Qaeda rejects it, and that international relief services are already overwhelmed by the unprecedented refugee crisis, and the human impact could be utterly horrendous even by comparison to what has happened. The most likely outcome would be a genocidal showdown between ISIS and the Shi'a militias. As recent Iraqi history has shown, however hard it might be to imagine that things could get worse, they most certainly can.

Second, the idea that a partition of Iraq would lead to viable, somehow more legitimate, Kurdish, Sunni and Shi'a mini-states is not supported by facts on the ground. Each of Iraq's regions has its intense internal conflicts, which the civil war has exacerbated, and (in historical terms) these regions – roughly speaking, the former Ottoman *vilayets* of Mosul, Baghdad and Basra – are just as cynical and artificial creations as Iraq itself, though of course they're creations of the Ottoman

Sultan rather than the European empires. Indeed, it was the very unsustainability of these Ottoman structures, and their lack of alignment with religious and ethnic realities on the ground, that prompted the nationalist revolts of World War I, which in turn led to the break-up of the Ottoman Empire and the creation of the modern Middle East. Thus, a break-up of Iraq would not create stable regions: rather, it would prompt massive instability, further Balkanisation and even more intense bloodshed. In effect, it would amount to exchanging one civil war for three: in Kurdistan, a delicate balance of power that has existed since the 1990s has been disrupted by the massive influx of Western weapons to fight ISIS; in southern Iraq, several well-armed Shi'a factions are at each others' throats and there's no clear regional authority; while in Anbar and other Sunni-majority areas, ISIS competes for control with Ba'athists, secular nationalists and tribal leaders.

Third, at the regional level (to paraphrase Ambassador James Jeffrey, one of the unsung heroes of American diplomacy in Iraq), once you start accepting the unravelling of the Sykes–Picot Agreement and the associated national boundaries created by Western powers after the world wars – which include the frontiers of Syria, Lebanon, Jordan, Israel, Egypt and modern Turkey – where do you stop? ISIS is, in large measure, motivated by an attempt to erase these boundaries and create a new Islamic caliphate in their stead. Even if it's too late to put Iraq back together, there are still excellent reasons to try to maintain a stable geopolitical framework in the Middle East. Failing to do so would indeed, in Professor Kessler's formulation, leave the rest of the world "worse off" and "hugely deprived" – not just because of the massive increase in an already overwhelming outflow of refugees (with strongly destabilising effects in Africa, Europe and Southeast Asia, and knock-on effects for boat arrivals in Australia) but also through enormous disruption to global transport and trade networks (which pass through the region and have a huge impact on Australia) and oil supplies (which, like it or not, still drive much of the world economy).

This also suggests a response to Hugh White's comments. He writes:

> Better, then, to leave the Iraqis and their neighbours to sort this one out without our help. That does not mean sitting back while ISIS takes over the Middle East, of course, because ISIS is already contained by the powers it has come up against – Turkey, the Kurds, Iraqi Shi'as and of course Iran, as well as Sunni rivals and adversaries inside and outside Iraq and Syria. These are the forces that will determine the shape of the new Middle East and ISIS's role in it, and there is not much that we in the West can do to shape the outcome.

The local and regional powers Professor White mentions, far from being able to contain ISIS, have unfortunately already proven they're utterly unable to do so without external assistance. Despite support from Iran and Hezbollah, Syria continues to lose ground to ISIS, as does Iraq. The success of Shi'a militias in re-taking Tikrit, and of the Kurds in stabilising their front near Irbil and staving off the fall of Kobani, were also heavily dependent on Western (mainly US) airpower and weapons. And as I argued in the essay, the choice is not between Western intervention and *no* intervention – rather, the danger is that in the absence of an international effort, conducted in accordance with international norms, the conflict will draw regional powers like Israel, Iran, Egypt, Saudi Arabia and Turkey into an increasingly savage confrontation. The escalating conflict in Yemen is just a taste of how this might look: again, while things seem bad now, they could get enormously worse – especially if we "leave Iraqis and their neighbours to sort this one out without our help."

Professor White's second point, however, is well taken – local and regional powers in the Middle East are indeed the "forces that will determine the shape of the new Middle East and ISIS's role in it," and Western countries can have, at best, a shaping role in enabling that process. As I argued in the essay, the attempt to remake the Middle East in our own image after 9/11 was a massive strategic error, on par with Hitler's invasion of Russia in 1941: a fundamentally misguided adventure whose consequences we'll be dealing with for generations. As Ali Allawi (former finance minister of Iraq and author of one of the most compelling critiques of the US-led occupation) has pointed out, the confrontation between Shi'a and Sunni across the Islamic world can be considered a Muslim equivalent of Europe's horrific and transformative Thirty Years' War. In that analogy, though, the West stands in the same relationship to the protagonists as the Ottoman Empire did to seventeenth-century Europe: an external player whose ability to shape any particular outcome is extremely limited.

This is what I take to be Paul McGeough's underlying argument when he writes that "in the Middle East, it's as though a history or foreign intervention is sufficient to justify more intervention, a sense that somehow it's okay to use other people's lives and homelands as laboratories for what might be a smart new Western idea. Merely testing the idea is enough; there is no recognition that by intervening you take on a huge duty of care to the poor buggers whose misfortune it is to live there." While his first point is, I think, completely correct – Western powers have indeed screwed this entire region up, over generations, by a series of ill-judged, often capricious, always self-interested interventions – they certainly had lots of extremely talented and dedicated help as they did so, from a collection of regional and local players of all stripes.

At the same time, I'm not sure that Paul himself fully accepts the implications of his second point, about the duty of care. This, in fact, was precisely my motivation for getting involved in Iraq, a conflict that I (like every other reputable student of guerrilla warfare) opposed from the outset. Regardless of how ill-advised it was to invade Iraq – and it most certainly was – once we did so, we took on a legal and moral responsibility for the Iraqi population that can't be wished away simply because it's now painful and inconvenient. Indeed, the fact that we ended up stuck with this responsibility is one of the main reasons why invading Iraq was such a bad idea in the first place. The issue now is how best to discharge that moral obligation (I agree with Audrey Cronin that it's no longer a legal obligation per se) without making things even worse.

Martin Chulov – like McGeough, one of print journalism's longest-serving and most perceptive observers of the Middle East – makes a similar point:

> if Humpty Dumpty is ever to be put back together, it will need more than all the king's horses and men. Nothing short of a grand bargain, bringing in all the region's stakeholders – Saudi Arabia, Iran, Turkey, Russia and the United States – is likely to generate real traction. All will need to recognise that mutually assured destruction awaits the region if a power-sharing compromise is not struck. To the extent that Obama has had a strategy, it has been about the nuclear deal – a good-faith test that could develop into a broader neighbourly role. So far, that has been an impossible sell to Saudi Arabia. And even a full-blown existential crisis may not change that.

I think Chulov is exactly right here. As I've mentioned, the nuclear deal has enabled a new US attempt to partner with Russia and Iran to resolve the Syrian conflict. This doesn't, of course, mean that peace is breaking out between these long-standing adversaries, but it does suggest an attempt at pragmatic cooperation around areas of shared interest. The problem with this approach lies not only in the possibility that Iran is negotiating in bad faith or may seek to expand its sponsorship of terrorism using newly available resources once sanctions are lifted. There's also the issue of how the nuclear deal looks from Tel Aviv, Riyadh, Cairo and Ankara – in other words, the reaction of regional players to the perceived rapprochement between their traditional ally and an enemy many see as promoting a destabilising, expansionist and sectarian agenda.

Waleed Aly makes a similar point, but then mounts what I think is the strong-est critique of my essay – namely, that Western politicians and populations simply lack the will, after all that's happened, to do what's needed to defeat ISIS. Speaking of Australia's decision to expand airstrikes into Syria in response to a US request, he writes:

> So we'll go. But what we almost certainly won't do is anything resembling what Kilcullen suggests in *Blood Year*. No "radically increased weight of air power" and certainly no "larger number of ground troops than at present – but under very different rules of engagement." Kilcullen is clearly as sceptical about this as I am, pointing to President Obama's foreign policy instinct to resist any-thing hawkish that isn't executed by remote control. The other widely acknowledged factor is simply that, for better or worse, we're over this stuff. Western nations are drained of the political will that would see them make a new blood sacrifice.

Audrey Cronin echoes Aly:

> Dave ends his essay maintaining that the most important thing is "the centrality of political will." I agree. But in Iraq, the political will of Western societies is secondary to the political will of the Ira-qis. I sincerely hope that the new Iraqi government will be able to rally its inhabitants – Shi'a and Sunni alike – to support and fight for it, especially with the help of aggressive American and Australian air power. But no matter how much equipment or how many embedded advisers we provide, external powers will never be able to *force* them to do so. War is, and always has been, a matter of clashing wills.

I'm sorry to say that these critiques, already quite persuasive last year, look even more compelling as time goes on. The chance of President Obama revers-ing the whole strategic tendency of his presidency, engaging in a wholehearted attempt to destroy ISIS as a state, taking action against Syria's continued large-scale use of chemical weapons, or contemplating the commitment of ground troops to the kinds of post-conflict stabilisation efforts that would be needed in the event of a peace deal, is next to nothing. And while US strategy remains unclear and non-committal, neither regional partners nor allies like Australia can or should get too far out in front. Similarly, the chance that Iraqi politicians will muster the political will to forge a robust enough consensus, or create an inclusive enough political process, to get sufficient Iraqis behind them to create the political basis for a successful campaign against ISIS is slim to non-existent.

Thus, the question – one that is, by definition, impossible to answer now, but which I plan to address in the book version of *Blood Year* – is what can be done within a broader framework of containment, how bad things could get before a new administration takes office in Washington, and what options might be open to the next president.

This speaks to the dilemma that James Brown highlights when he writes:

> Kilcullen identifies the impossible task that voters set for leaders – guarantee us perfect safety from terrorism, but within the constraints of a liberal democracy governed by the rule of law. Little has changed in this regard since the attacks in New York of 2001. Governments cannot inoculate us against every ill, nor stop every terrorist madly committed to the destruction of an Australian target. But our rule of law is precious, worth defending, and even worth risking our lives for. Someday the seemingly unstoppable momentum of ISIS will abate. We must be careful that we don't spend too much of what we truly value in order to bring ISIS down.

And this is the area where, if anything, events have moved fastest since I wrote the essay, and where the issues are starker than ever. The beach massacre at Sousse, Tunisia, that killed thirty-eight tourists (thirty of whom were British), the flood of refugees into Europe that prompted anti-immigrant riots in Germany in August 2015, the spate of ISIS-inspired terrorist attacks in the United States, Europe, Turkey, Egypt and elsewhere, and the growth of ISIS *wilayats* across North Africa, South Asia and the Caucasus shows that this problem is no longer confined to the Middle East, but has well and truly come home to roost. In the atmosphere of moral panic occasioned by the renewed threat of terrorism, the risk that we'll sign on the dotted line, giving up precious liberties impossible to recover in the name of safety, is ever-present. But as Benjamin Franklin wrote in 1775, "Those who would give up essential Liberty, to purchase a little temporary Safety, deserve neither Liberty nor Safety."

As I explained in the essay, the threat of ISIS doesn't presently justify such a response at home. The Islamic State doesn't (or doesn't yet) pose a large-scale terrorism threat to Western countries. On the contrary, the most distinctive thing about ISIS is that it's a state-building enterprise and, increasingly, a state-like entity: one with a radically revolutionary agenda that seeks to destroy the nation-state system in the Middle East, replace it with a theocratic caliphate, and then launch a millenarian, genocidal conquest for territory and population. ISIS's ability to reach into our own societies, to radicalise and operationalise discontented and marginalised individuals, is an irritant now, but would create a deadly Fifth Column in that event.

Thus, for now, the task is to confront ISIS overseas, lest we be forced (or tricked, or persuaded) to turn our societies into police states. If defeating the group at its source is not feasible – for the excellent reason, advanced by Waleed Aly and Audrey Cronin, that people are just not willing to commit to it – then some form of active containment may be the best we can do for the moment. But let's be under no illusion that such an approach will ultimately solve this problem – which, as I've explained, is largely one of our own making. If we don't go to ISIS, they are most assuredly coming to us.

David Kilcullen

Waleed Aly is a presenter of *The Project* and a lecturer in politics at Monash University. He is the author of Quarterly Essay 37, *What's Right? The Future of Conservatism in Australia*, and *People Like Us: How Arrogance is Dividing Islam and The West*.

James Brown is the author of *Anzac's Long Shadow*. A former Australian Army officer, he commanded a cavalry troop in southern Iraq and served on the Australian task-force in Baghdad. He is the director of the US Studies Centre's Alliance 21 project.

Martin Chulov is the *Guardian's* Middle East correspondent. In 2015 he won the Orwell Prize for journalism.

Audrey Kurth Cronin is distinguished professor at George Mason University. Her books include *How Terrorism Ends: Understanding the Decline and Demise of Terrorist Campaigns*.

Clive Kessler is emeritus professor of sociology and anthropology at the University of New South Wales.

David Kilcullen was a senior advisor to General David Petraeus in 2007 and 2008, when he helped to design and monitor the Iraq War coalition troop "Surge." He has also been an adviser to the UK and Australian governments, NATO and the International Security Assistance Force. He is the author of *The Accidental Guerrilla, Counterinsurgency* and *Out of the Mountains*.

David Marr is the author of *Patrick White: A Life, Panic, The High Price of Heaven* and *Dark Victory* (with Marian Wilkinson). He has written for the *Sydney Morning Herald*, the *Age*, the *Saturday Paper*, the *Guardian* and the *Monthly*, and been editor of the *National Times*, a reporter for *Four Corners* and presenter of ABC TV's *Media Watch*. He is the author of four previous bestselling Quarterly Essays.

Paul McGeough is the Washington-based chief correspondent for Fairfax and the author of Quarterly Essay 14, *Mission Impossible: The Sheikhs, the US and the Future of Iraq*.

Jim Molan served as chief of operations of the Headquarters Multinational Force in Iraq. He is the author of *Running the War in Iraq*.

Hugh White is the author of Quarterly Essay 39, *Power Shift: Australia's Future between Washington and Beijing*. He is a professor of strategic studies at ANU and a visiting fellow at the Lowy Institute.

SUBSCRIBE to Quarterly Ess
SAVE over 35% on the cover p

Subscriptions: Receive a discount and never miss an issue. Mailed direct to your
☐ **1 year subscription** (4 issues): $59 within Australia incl. GST. Outside Australia $89.
☐ **2 year subscription** (8 issues): $105 within Australia incl. GST. Outside Australia $165
* All prices include postage and handling.

Back Issues: (Prices include postage and handling.)

☐ **QE 2** ($15.99) John Birmingham *Appeasing Jakarta*
☐ **QE 4** ($15.99) Don Watson *Rabbit Syndrome*
☐ **QE 6** ($15.99) John Button *Beyond Belief*
☐ **QE 7** ($15.99) John Martinkus *Paradise Betrayed*
☐ **QE 8** ($15.99) Amanda Lohrey *Groundswell*
☐ **QE 10** ($15.99) Gideon Haigh *Bad Company*
☐ **QE 11** ($15.99) Germaine Greer *Whitefella Jump Up*
☐ **QE 12** ($15.99) David Malouf *Made in England*
☐ **QE 13** ($15.99) Robert Manne with David Corlett *Sending Them Home*
☐ **QE 14** ($15.99) Paul McGeough *Mission Impossible*
☐ **QE 15** ($15.99) Margaret Simons *Latham's World*
☐ **QE 17** ($15.99) John Hirst *"Kangaroo Court"*
☐ **QE 18** ($15.99) Gail Bell *The Worried Well*
☐ **QE 19** ($15.99) Judith Brett *Relaxed & Comfortable*
☐ **QE 20** ($15.99) John Birmingham *A Time for War*
☐ **QE 21** ($15.99) Clive Hamilton *What's Left?*
☐ **QE 22** ($15.99) Amanda Lohrey *Voting for Jesus*
☐ **QE 23** ($15.99) Inga Clendinnen *The History Question*
☐ **QE 24** ($15.99) Robyn Davidson *No Fixed Address*
☐ **QE 25** ($15.99) Peter Hartcher *Bipolar Nation*
☐ **QE 26** ($15.99) David Marr *His Master's Voice*
☐ **QE 27** ($15.99) Ian Lowe *Reaction Time*
☐ **QE 28** ($15.99) Judith Brett *Exit Right*
☐ **QE 29** ($15.99) Anne Manne *Love & Money*
☐ **QE 30** ($15.99) Paul Toohey *Last Drinks*

☐ **QE 31** ($15.99) Tim Flannery *Now or Never*
☐ **QE 32** ($15.99) Kate Jennings *American Revolution*
☐ **QE 33** ($15.99) Guy Pearse *Quarry Vision*
☐ **QE 34** ($15.99) Annabel Crabb *Stop at Nothing*
☐ **QE 36** ($15.99) Mungo MacCallum *Australian Story*
☐ **QE 37** ($15.99) Waleed Aly *What's Right?*
☐ **QE 38** ($15.99) David Marr *Power Trip*
☐ **QE 39** ($15.99) Hugh White *Power Shift*
☐ **QE 42** ($15.99) Judith Brett *Fair Share*
☐ **QE 43** ($15.99) Robert Manne *Bad News*
☐ **QE 44** ($15.99) Andrew Charlton *Man-Made World*
☐ **QE 45** ($15.99) Anna Krien *Us and Them*
☐ **QE 46** ($15.99) Laura Tingle *Great Expectations*
☐ **QE 47** ($15.99) David Marr *Political Animal*
☐ **QE 48** ($15.99) Tim Flannery *After the Future*
☐ **QE 49** ($15.99) Mark Latham *Not Dead Yet*
☐ **QE 50** ($15.99) Anna Goldsworthy *Unfinished Business*
☐ **QE 51** ($15.99) David Marr *The Prince*
☐ **QE 52** ($15.99) Linda Jaivin *Found in Translation*
☐ **QE 53** ($15.99) Paul Toohey *That Sinking Feeling*
☐ **QE 54** ($15.99) Andrew Charlton *Dragon's Tail*
☐ **QE 55** ($15.99) Noel Pearson *A Rightful Place*
☐ **QE 56** ($15.99) Guy Rundle *Clivosaurus*
☐ **QE 57** ($15.99) Karen Hitchcock *Dear Life*
☐ **QE 58** ($15.99) David Kilcullen *Blood Year*

Payment Details: I enclose a cheque/money order made out to Schwartz Publishing Pty Ltd.
Please debit my credit card (Mastercard or Visa accepted).

Card No. ☐☐☐☐ ☐☐☐☐ ☐☐☐☐ ☐☐☐☐

Expiry date / **CCV** **Amount $**

Cardholder's name **Signature**

Name

Addressd

Email **Phone**

Post or fax this form to: Quarterly Essay, Reply Paid 79448, Collingwood VIC 3066 /
Tel: (03) 9486 0288 / Fax: (03) 9486 0244 / Email: subscribe@blackincbooks.com
Subscribe online at **www.quarterlyessay.com**